Israel

OPPOSING VIEWPOINTS®

Israel

OPPOSING VIEWPOINTS®

Other Books of Related Interest

Israel

OPPOSING VIEWPOINTS®

John Woodward, *Book Editor*

Bruce Glassman, *Vice President*
Bonnie Szumski, *Publisher*
Helen Cothran, *Managing Editor*

OPPOSING
VIEWPOINTS®
SERIES

GREENHAVEN PRESS

An imprint of Thomson Gale, a part of The Thomson Corporation

THOMSON

———✳———™

GALE

Detroit • New York • San Francisco • San Diego • New Haven, Conn.
Waterville, Maine • London • Munich

THOMSON

GALE

LIBRARY OF CONGRESS CATALOGING-IN-PUBLICATION DATA

Israel / John Woodward, book editor.
    p. cm. — (Opposing viewpoints series)
Includes bibliographical references and index.
ISBN 0-7377-2589-3 (lib. : alk. paper) — ISBN 0-7377-2590-7 (pbk. : alk. paper)
    1. Arab-Israeli conflict. 2. Zionism—History. 3. Palestinian Arabs—Ethnic identity. 4. United States—Foreign relations—Middle East. 5. Middle East—Foreign relations—United States. I. Woodward, John. II. Opposing viewpoints series (Unnumbered)
DS119.7.I775 2005
956.9405—dc22
    2004060586

Printed in the United States of America

"Congress shall make
no law. . . abridging the
freedom of speech, or of
the press."

First Amendment to the U.S. Constitution

The basic foundation of our democracy is the First
Amendment guarantee of freedom of expression.
The Opposing Viewpoints Series is dedicated to the
concept of this basic freedom and the idea that it is
more important to practice it than to enshrine it.

Contents

Why Consider Opposing Viewpoints?

"The only way in which a human being can make some approach to knowing the whole of a subject is by hearing what can be said about it by persons of every variety of opinion and studying all modes in which it can be looked at by every character of mind. No wise man ever acquired his wisdom in any mode but this."

John Stuart Mill

In our media-intensive culture it is not difficult to find differing opinions. Thousands of newspapers and magazines and dozens of radio and television talk shows resound with differing points of view. The difficulty lies in deciding which opinion to agree with and which "experts" seem the most credible. The more inundated we become with differing opinions and claims, the more essential it is to hone critical reading and thinking skills to evaluate these ideas. Opposing Viewpoints books address this problem directly by presenting stimulating debates that can be used to enhance and teach these skills. The varied opinions contained in each book examine many different aspects of a single issue. While examining these conveniently edited opposing views, readers can develop critical thinking skills such as the ability to compare and contrast authors' credibility, facts, argumentation styles, use of persuasive techniques, and other stylistic tools. In short, the Opposing Viewpoints Series is an ideal way to attain the higher-level thinking and reading skills so essential in a culture of diverse and contradictory opinions.

In addition to providing a tool for critical thinking, Opposing Viewpoints books challenge readers to question their own strongly held opinions and assumptions. Most people form their opinions on the basis of upbringing, peer pressure, and personal, cultural, or professional bias. By reading carefully balanced opposing views, readers must directly confront new ideas as well as the opinions of those with whom they disagree. This is not to simplistically argue that

11

everyone who reads opposing views will—or should—change his or her opinion. Instead, the series enhances readers' understanding of their own views by encouraging confrontation with opposing ideas. Careful examination of others' views can lead to the readers' understanding of the logical inconsistencies in their own opinions, perspective on why they hold an opinion, and the consideration of the possibility that their opinion requires further evaluation.

Evaluating Other Opinions

To ensure that this type of examination occurs, Opposing Viewpoints books present all types of opinions. Prominent spokespeople on different sides of each issue as well as well-known professionals from many disciplines challenge the reader. An additional goal of the series is to provide a forum for other, less known, or even unpopular viewpoints. The opinion of an ordinary person who has had to make the decision to cut off life support from a terminally ill relative, for example, may be just as valuable and provide just as much insight as a medical ethicist's professional opinion. The editors have two additional purposes in including these less known views. One, the editors encourage readers to respect others' opinions—even when not enhanced by professional credibility. It is only by reading or listening to and objectively evaluating others' ideas that one can determine whether they are worthy of consideration. Two, the inclusion of such viewpoints encourages the important critical thinking skill of objectively evaluating an author's credentials and bias. This evaluation will illuminate an author's reasons for taking a particular stance on an issue and will aid in readers' evaluation of the author's ideas.

It is our hope that these books will give readers a deeper understanding of the issues debated and an appreciation of the complexity of even seemingly simple issues when good and honest people disagree. This awareness is particularly important in a democratic society such as ours in which people enter into public debate to determine the common good. Those with whom one disagrees should not be regarded as enemies but rather as people whose views deserve careful examination and may shed light on one's own.

Thomas Jefferson once said that "difference of opinion leads to inquiry, and inquiry to truth." Jefferson, a broadly educated man, argued that "if a nation expects to be ignorant and free . . . it expects what never was and never will be." As individuals and as a nation, it is imperative that we consider the opinions of others and examine them with skill and discernment. The Opposing Viewpoints Series is intended to help readers achieve this goal.

David L. Bender and Bruno Leone,
Founders

Greenhaven Press anthologies primarily consist of previously published material taken from a variety of sources, including periodicals, books, scholarly journals, newspapers, government documents, and position papers from private and public organizations. These original sources are often edited for length and to ensure their accessibility for a young adult audience. The anthology editors also change the original titles of these works in order to clearly present the main thesis of each viewpoint and to explicitly indicate the opinion presented in the viewpoint. These alterations are made in consideration of both the reading and comprehension levels of a young adult audience. Every effort is made to ensure that Greenhaven Press accurately reflects the original intent of the authors included in this anthology.

Introduction

"The Palestinian woman's womb is the only womb I know of that has been inhumanely described as a 'dormant explosive bomb.'"

—Samah Jabr

Israel's past has been shaped by changing demographics, and its future will likely be as well. Israeli scholars claim that there has been a Jewish presence in Palestine for thousands of years. According to Jewish tradition, the unified nation of Israel in Palestine first came into being about 1000 B.C., but the Jews were driven into exile by the Romans in the first century A.D. This dispersion of the Jews is referred to as the Diaspora. The primary mission of Zionism was to call home the Diaspora Jews into a newly re-created Israel in their traditional homeland. Thus, one of the most fundamental of modern Israel's Basic Laws is the Law of Return, which grants full citizenship to any Jew who wishes to immigrate to Israel. David Ben-Gurion, Israel's first prime minister, said, "This is not only a Jewish state, where the majority of the inhabitants are Jews, but a state for all Jews, wherever they are, and for every Jew who wants to be here. . . . This right is inherent in being a Jew."

Israel's Jewish population was built on the concept of aliyah, the return of the Diaspora Jews to their homeland in Palestine. There have been seven main periods of aliyah. The first occurred between 1882 and 1903, when the Zionist movement first organized and land was purchased in Palestine for Jewish settlers. Most of these first immigrants came from Russia. The second aliyah was between 1904 and 1914. Most of these immigrants came from Russia and Poland. The third aliyah occurred between 1919 and 1923, again with most coming from Russia. The fourth aliyah involved immigrants from Poland and lasted from 1924 to 1932. German Jews, driven by the urgent need to escape the increasingly oppressive, anti-Semitic Nazi regime, immigrated in the fifth aliyah between 1933 and 1939. After Israel declared its independence in 1948, there was massive Jewish immigration from throughout Europe and Arab countries. Most recently, the breakup of the Soviet Union in 1989 also led to the immigration of large numbers of Soviet Jews.

Jews have also arrived from Africa. Israel has twice managed a large-scale exodus of Jews from Ethiopia. Between 1977 and 1984, approximately 8,000 Ethiopian Jews were brought to Israel via covert actions. Another 8,000 Ethiopians were airlifted to Israel during Operation Moses, which was launched on November 19, 1984, and ended on January 5, 1985. Finally, Operation Solomon began on Friday, May 24, 1991. For thirty-six hours, thirty-six El Al jumbo jets and C-130 cargo planes carried the 14,324 remaining Ethiopian Jews to their new home in Israel.

There are still Jews who "make aliyah" to Israel each year, but not on the scale of previous years. Since large Jewish immigration waves are no longer likely, Arab and Jewish birthrates now have the greatest demographic impact on Israel. former Palestinian Authority chairman Yasir Arafat was frequently reported to refer to the "weapon of the womb," meaning the high birthrate among Palestinian women. The Palestinian birthrate is 5.9 per woman, far higher than the 2.9 of Israeli Jews. Israel's Arab citizens, currently about 20 percent of the population, also have a higher birthrate of 4.7. With Arab birthrates higher than Jewish birthrates, many analysts predict that Israel will inevitably lose its Jewish majority and will become dominated by Arabs.

There are several potential futures for Israel, all driven by demography. If Israel were to annex the West Bank, which is heavily populated with Palestinians, to create a "greater Israel," the Jewish population of the country would decline from the current 80 percent to 51 percent. By 2020 this percentage would likely drop to 42 percent, which means there will be more Arabs than Jews between the Jordan River and the Mediterranean Sea. Some advocate this one-state approach, which would transform Israel into a binational or even a Muslim state, as the solution to the Israeli-Palestinian conflict. Others believe the only way to end the conflict and preserve the Jewish nature of Israel is the creation of a Palestinian state in the West Bank and Gaza. However, the Palestinians to date have insisted upon the "right of return" of

Palestinian refugees, meaning the right of refugees displaced in 1948 and their descendants to return to Israel. This would add millions of Arabs to the Israeli population and completely change the nature of the country.

Even if the "right of return" is dropped as a condition for a peace agreement, however, some Jews remain concerned that the growing Arab population already within Israel is a demographic ticking time bomb. According to the Jewish Agency for Israel, "Because of the rapid natural increase of the Palestinian population, it is expected that the percentage of the Jewish population within Israel will drop to 68% by 2020, despite continuing immigration to the country." As a result, there are calls from some in the Knesset (the Israeli parliament) for removing all Arabs from Israel and transferring them to the occupied territories, a future Palestinian state, or other Arab state, such as Jordan. Many denounce this idea as "ethnic cleansing."

Israel's history is a story of demographic transformation, and demographics will also determine its future. Israel is the only nation in which Jews are a majority. Most Israeli Jews believe that a Muslim majority in the state of Israel will fundamentally change its nature, relegating Jews to a minority in their own state, forced to once again endure the discrimination they suffered as minorities in other states. Others, however, believe that the Jews and Palestinians can learn to peacefully coexist in a single state, much as different racial and ethnic groups have learned to live together in the West.

Whether Israel can survive is one of the important questions debated in *Opposing Viewpoints: Israel* in the following chapters: Should Israel Exist? What Are the Roots of the Israeli-Palestinian Conflict? Is Peace Between Israel and the Palestinians Possible? What Should U.S. Policy Be Toward Israel? The diverse viewpoints in this book will help readers to understand the complex issues facing Israel and its neighbors.

CHAPTER 1

Should Israel Exist?

Chapter Preface

Israel was founded as a Jewish state, but when the nation's first prime minister, David Ben-Gurion, declared Israel's independence in 1948, he did not specifically mention Judaism. Some commentators believe that Israel's founding was only a nationalist act, the return of a displaced ethnic group to its ancestral home. Others contend that Judaism is central to the state's creation. At the heart of the issue is the question of what role religion was intended to play in Israel. In the United States, religious freedom and the separation of church and state were clearly established in the First Amendment to the Constitution. However, one cannot examine Israel's constitution to look for similar declarations; no constitution has yet been written. Israeli law states that Israel is a Jewish state and that freedom of religion is protected; however, this apparent contradiction generates controversy even today.

Indeed, there is a continuing debate within the nation about the importance of Judaism to Israel and about the role religion should play in government. According to Israeli government statistics, approximately 80 percent of the nation's population of 6.4 million is Jewish, but half of Israeli Jews consider themselves to be secular. Other faiths represented in Israel include Muslim, Christian, and Druze. Many of these citizens complain that Israel is more theocracy than democracy; however, its parliament—the Knesset—as well as the positions of prime minister and president, are modeled on the secular European model.

The Israeli government, through its Ministry for Religious Affairs, manages religious life in Israel. It is responsible for the construction and maintenance of religious structures and has oversight responsibility for cemeteries and burials. It also provides funding for a variety of religious organizations and activities, such as parochial schools, but funds are not distributed equally, and this is a source of resentment among religious minorities. According to the U.S. State Department's 2001 International Religious Freedom Report, "The [Israeli] Government funds both religious and secular schools in the country, including non-Jewish religious and secular schools . . . [but] schools in Arab areas, including Arab parochial schools, receive significantly fewer resources than comparable Jewish schools."

Many Israeli Jews are unhappy with the influence of religion on the government. Despite being practiced by only 17.5 percent of the population, Orthodox Judaism permeates Israeli government and society. Orthodox Jewish religious authorities have exclusive control over Jewish marriages, divorces, and most burials. Controversially, the Orthodox authorities do not recognize marriages or conversions to Judaism performed in Israel by Conservative or Reform rabbis.

The Orthodox influence extends beyond religious life, as well. In deference to Orthodox beliefs, El Al, the national airline, as well as buses in most cities, do not operate on the Jewish Sabbath. In addition, although most men and single women are required to serve in the Israeli Defense Forces (IDF) at age eighteen, Orthodox women may be exempted. Most ultra-Orthodox men are granted deferments while pursuing Torah studies, and those who eventually do serve in the IDF mainly fulfill religious rather than combat functions. Many secular or Reform Jewish citizens understandably object to Orthodox influence and preferential treatment, causing increased conflict in Israeli society.

Israel is increasingly a fractured, Balkanized society. In addition to struggling with the continuing conflict with the Palestinians, the Jewish state is forced to acknowledge the reality that religion continues to divide Jew from Muslim, Christian, and Druze, as well as secular Jew from Orthodox. How Israel will manage to survive as a cohesive nation under such circumstances remains to be seen. In the following chapter, thinkers from across the political spectrum debate the Jewish nature of the state of Israel, its future, and the question of its very existence.

> *"Israel's founders—like the homesteaders in the American West—earned ownership to the land by developing it."*

Israel Has a Right to Exist

Yaron Brook and Peter Schwartz

In the following viewpoint, Yaron Brook and Peter Schwartz contend that Israel earned the right to the land it occupies by settling and developing it. Moreover, the authors argue that because it is a democracy, Israel is the only nation in the Middle East with moral legitimacy. Yaron Brook is executive director and Peter Schwartz is chairman of the board of directors of the Ayn Rand Institute, which promotes the philosophy of author Ayn Rand.

As you read, consider the following questions:

1. According to the authors, why is Israel justified in safeguarding itself against attack?
2. What do the authors believe is the goal of the Palestinians?
3. How do the authors compare Israel's situation with America's war on terrorism?

As yet another appalling suicide bombing takes place in Israel, killing 19 people and wounding dozens more on a bus packed with schoolchildren in Jerusalem—as Hamas claims credit for the massacre—America's policymakers still insist on seeking an "even-handed," diplomatic solution.

In the past 18 months [from December 2000 through June 2002], Israel's six million citizens have suffered 12,480 terrorist attacks. They have buried more than 400 victims—a per-capita death toll six times that of America on September 11 [2001]. Yet, in an abhorrent act of injustice, Israel continues to be pressured by the United States into making concessions to [Palestinian ruler] Yasser Arafat, the archpatron of those terror attacks. In the long run, this means that Israel is being pressured into sacrificing its basic right to exist.

We should be supporting Israel's right to take whatever military action is needed to defend itself against its nihilistic enemies. Morally and militarily, Israel is America's frontline in the war on terrorism. If America is swayed by Arafat's latest empty rhetoric, and allows him to continue threatening Israel, our own campaign against terrorism becomes sheer hypocrisy and will, ultimately, fail.

Consider the facts and judge for yourself:

The Israelis and the Palestinians Are Not Morally Equal

Israel is the only free country in a region dominated by Arab monarchies, theocracies and dictatorships. It is only the citizens of Israel—Arabs and Jews alike—who enjoy the right to express their views, to criticize their government, to form political parties, to publish private newspapers, to hold free elections. When Arab authorities deny the most basic freedoms to their own people, it is obscene for them to start claiming that Israel is violating the Palestinians' rights. All Arab citizens who are genuinely concerned with human rights should, as their very first action, seek to oust their own despotic rulers and adopt the type of free society that characterizes Israel.

Since its founding in 1948, Israel has had to fight five wars—all in self-defense—against 22 hostile Arab dictatorships, and has been repeatedly attacked by Palestinian terrorists. Arafat is responsible for the kidnapping and murder of Israeli schoolchildren, the hijacking of airliners and the car bombings and death-squad killings of thousands of Israeli, American, Lebanese and Palestinian civilians. Today he ardently sponsors such terror groups as Hamas, Islamic Jihad and the al-Aksa Brigade.

The land Israel is "occupying" was captured in a war initiated by its Arab neighbors. Like any victim of aggression, Israel has a moral right to control as much land as is necessary to safeguard itself against attack. The Palestinians want to annihilate Israel, while Israel wants simply to be left alone. If there is a moral failing on Israel's part, it consists of its reluctance to take *stronger* military measures. If it is right for America to bomb al-Qaeda [terrorist] strongholds in Afghanistan—and it is—then it is equally justifiable for Israel to bomb the terrorist strongholds in the occupied territories.

Hatred of Israel, and of the United States, Is Hatred for Western Values

Like America's war against the Taliban and al-Qaeda, the Arab-Israeli dispute is a conflict between opposing philosophies. On the one side are the forces of mysticism, medieval tribalism, dictatorship—and terror; on the other side are the forces of reason, individualism, capitalism—and civilization. Arafat and his sympathizers hate Israel for the same reason that Osama bin Laden and his sympathizers hate America, i.e., for embracing secular, Western values. No "peace process" is possible with such enemies.

This is not an ethnic battle between Jews and Arabs, but a moral battle between those who value the individual's right to be free and those who don't. Those Arabs who value individual freedom are enemies of the Arafat regime and deserve to be embraced by Israel; those Jews who do not value individual freedom deserve to be condemned by Israel.

Israelis Have a Right to the Land

Only Israel has a moral right to establish a government in that area—on the grounds, not of some ethnic or religious heritage, but of a secular, rational principle. Only a state based on political and economic freedom has moral legitimacy. Contrary to what the Palestinians are seeking, there can be no "right" to establish a dictatorship.

Israel Does Not Need Recognition of Its Right to Exist

Nobody does Israel any service by proclaiming its "right to exist." Israel's right to exist, like that of the United States, Saudi Arabia and 152 other states, is axiomatic and unreserved. Israel's legitimacy is not suspended in midair awaiting acknowledgement. . . .

There is certainly no other state, big or small, young or old, that would consider mere recognition of its "right to exist" a favor, or a negotiable concession.

Abba Eban, *New York Times*, November 18, 1981.

As to the rightful owners of particular pieces of property, Israel's founders—like the homesteaders in the American West—earned ownership to the land by developing it. They arrived in a desolate, sparsely populated region and drained the swamps, irrigated the desert, grew crops and built cities. They worked unclaimed land or purchased it from the owners. They introduced industry, libraries, hospitals, art galleries, universities—and the concept of individual rights. Those Arabs who abandoned their land in order to join the military crusade against Israel forfeited all right to their property. And if there are any peaceful Arabs who were forcibly evicted from their property, they should be entitled to press their claims in the courts of Israel, which, unlike the Arab autocracies, has an independent, objective judiciary—a judiciary that recognizes the principle of property rights.

Palestinians Are Not "Freedom Fighters"

The Palestinians want a state, not to secure their freedom, but to perpetuate the dictatorial reign of Arafat's Palestinian Authority. Arafat's "police" brutally expropriate property and silence opposing viewpoints by shutting down radio and TV stations. They systematically arrest, torture and murder peaceful dissenters. To call the militant Palestinians "freedom fighters"—when they support the subjugation of their own people, when they deliberately murder children in the streets

23

or gleefully praise such depravity—is a mind-numbing perversion.

In 1947 the Palestinians rejected the U.N.'s [United Nation's] offer of a state larger than the one they are demanding now. Instead, they joined in a war aimed at wiping Israel from the map. Today, that hostility has only hardened. For example, in a televised public sermon, a Palestinian Imam declared: "God willing, this unjust state [of] Israel, will be erased." Palestinian textbooks are filled with vile, anti-Jewish propaganda, such as this exhortation from a fifth-grade Arabic language text: "The Jihad against the Jew is the religious duty of every Muslim man and woman."

A Palestinian state headed by Arafat would be a launching pad and a training ground for terrorist organizations targeting, not only Israel, but the United States. Forcing Israelis to accept a Palestinian state under Arafat is like forcing Americans to accept a state the size of Mexico, 12 miles from New York City, ruled by Osama bin Laden. As long as the Palestinians sanction aggression, they should not be permitted their own state.

No rhetoric by Arafat can change the fact that he is a hater of freedom and a destroyer of innocent human life. Imagine Osama bin Laden being enticed by American diplomats to announce: "We strongly condemn operations that target American civilians, especially the last one in New York. We equally condemn the massacres that have been, and are still being, committed by U.S. occupation troops against Taliban civilians in Kandahar, Shah-i-Kot and Tora Bora." Would any sane individual thereby endorse an immediate withdrawal of U.S. forces from Afghanistan and the creation of a Taliban state, headed by bin Laden, alongside America? If not, why should Israel be expected to act so suicidally?

America Must Allow Israel to Uphold the Principle of Self-Defense

The growing demand for Israel to negotiate with Arafat comes from an unprincipled, range-of-the-moment mentality. Surrendering to extortion—which the "land-for-peace" catechism endorses—is profoundly immoral and impractical. In the 1938 version of "land for peace," Nazi Germany was appeased by being allowed to take over Czechoslovakia as part of the Aryan people's "homeland"; the result was to encourage Hitler to start a world war. The Arab-Israeli conflict could become a dress rehearsal for a wider, global conflict. If America now stops Israel from retaliating against Arafat, the father of international terrorism, how can it ever justify retaliation against its own enemies? If we force Israel to appease Arafat, we will be broadcasting, loud and clear, that terrorism can bring America to its knees.

We should urge our government to recognize that there is only one means of achieving long-term Mideast peace: upholding the principle of a free society, which entails the endorsement of Israel's sweeping retaliation against the scourge of terrorism.

"The Zionist State known as 'Israel' is a regime that has no right to exist."

Israel Has No Right to Exist

Ahron Cohen

The following viewpoint was originally given as a talk in the United Kingdom on July 28, 2002, under the auspices of the Islamic Human Rights Commission. In it Ahron Cohen argues that Zionism—the movement to establish a Jewish state in Palestine—is contrary to Judaism. He believes that the creation of Israel represents an abandonment of the values of the Jewish faith, which hold that the Jewish Diaspora was ordained by God as punishment for not living appropriately. Cohen believes Jews should live in other nations and abandon Israel to the Palestinians. Ahron Cohen is an Orthodox rabbi.

As you read, consider the following questions:
1. According to the author, how have Zionists treated the Arabs?
2. What does the author want for Israel's future?
3. According to the author, why exactly were the Jewish people exiled?

Ahron Cohen, "Orthodox Jews Condemn Zionism," speech at Luton Bedfordshire, UK, July 28, 2002, under the auspices of the Islamic Human Rights Commission. Reproduced by permission. www.netureikarta.org.

M y friends!
We are here today to protest against the terrible
wrongs being perpetrated against the Palestinian People by
the Zionist illegitimate regime in Palestine.

I am an orthodox Jew involved in ecclesiastical duties
within the Jewish Community.

I am particularly involved in educating our youth.

How do I come to be here today? Let me explain.

My qualification to talk to you today is basically by virtue
of my being one of many orthodox Jews who completely
sympathise with your cause. The spearhead group among us
who are involved actively in this matter on a regular basis are
called Neturei Karta, which can be loosely translated as
Guardians of the faith.

Representatives of Neturei Karta take part in protests,
which draw attention to Arab and Muslim pain, whenever
they can. The Neturei Karta would like to express its solidarity with its Muslim brothers and explain the following points:
The ideology of Zionism and its practical outcome in the
form of the State known as 'Israel' is completely alien to Judaism and the Jewish faith.

The apparent connection between Judaism and Zionism
is false. The connection has been nurtured by the Zionists in
order to ensnare as many Jews as possible within their net.
The very name "Israel" which originally meant what are
known as the Children of Israel i.e. the Jewish People was
usurped by the Zionists. For this reason many orthodox Jews
avoid referring to the Zionist State by the name 'Israel'.

The Zionists have made themselves to appear as the representatives and spokespeople of all Jews thus, because of
their actions, arousing animosity against the Jews. But, this
is simply not true! Zionism is not Judaism. Zionists cannot
speak in the name of Jews.

Zionism in general and its conduct against the Arabs,
Muslims and wider world is totally contrary to the teachings
of the religion, beliefs and hopes of the Jewish people.

Jewish Exile

For the last two thousand years or so the Jewish people have
been in a state of exile decreed by the Almighty. The Jews

were exiled from their land because they did not maintain the standards expected of them. This state of exile is the situation that exists right up to the present day. It is a basic part of our belief to accept willingly the Heavenly decree of exile and not to try and fight against it. In practical terms, exile for us means that Jews must be loyal subjects of the countries in which they live and not attempt to rule over the established indigenous populations of those countries. And of course this includes Palestine.

Permanent War

While Israel continues to exist, it will be permanently at war with the indigenous Palestinians who wish to return home. The only rational way of ending the bloodshed is for the replacement of the Zionist state with a democratic, secular state in Palestine, which guarantees the rights of all minorities, whatever their religion or ethnicity.

Sue Boland, *Green Left Weekly*, April 25, 2000.

The Zionist movement founded approximately 100 years ago based on secular nationalistic aims was a complete abandonment of our religious teachings and faith—in general—and in particular regarding our approach to the peoples among whom we live.

It follows, therefore, that the Jewish people have no right to rule today in Palestine.

The Palestinians Own Palestine

According to the Torah and Jewish faith, the present Palestinian Arab claim to rule in Palestine is right and just. The Zionist claim is wrong and criminal.

One must add to this wrong, the fact that in order to achieve an ill conceived nationalistic ambition, a shocking contravention of natural justice was committed by the Zionists in setting up an illegitimate regime in Palestine completely against the wishes of the established population, the Palestinians, which inevitably had to be based on loss of life, killing and stealing.

We want to tell the world, especially our Muslim neighbours, that there is no hatred or animosity between Jew and

Muslim. We wish to live together as friends and neighbours as we have done mostly over hundreds even thousands of years in all the Arab countries. It was only the advent of the Zionists and Zionism which upset this age old relationship.

Zionism Is a Tragedy

The Zionist oppression, abuse and murder of Arabs is a tragedy not only for the Palestinians but for the Jewish people as well.

It must therefore be clear that opposition to Zionism and its crimes does not imply hatred of Jews. On the contrary Zionism itself and its deeds are the biggest threat to Judaism. Zionism hates Judaism. Zionism has turned many Jewish believers into atheists and warmongers.

Together we must work so as not to allow the Zionists to fuel the fires of hatred between Arab and Jew. That is what they want and we must not let them succeed.

The Zionist State known as "Israel" is a regime that has no right to exist. Its continuing existence is the underlying cause of the strife in Palestine.

We pray for a solution to the terrible and tragic impasse that exists. Hopefully based on results brought about by moral, political and economic pressures imposed by the nations of the world.

We pray for an end to bloodshed, an end to the suffering of our Palestinian brethren and all innocent people worldwide.

We are waiting for the annulment of Zionism and the dismantling of the Zionist regime, and would welcome the opportunity to dwell in peace in the holy land under a rule which is entirely in accordance with the wishes and aspirations of the Palestinian People.

May we soon merit the time when all mankind will be at peace with each other.

"The State of Israel is the national home of the Jewish people."

Israel Should Remain a Jewish State

Forum for National Responsibility

In the following viewpoint, the Forum for National Responsibility argues that Israel should remain a Jewish state and the national homeland of the Jewish people. The authors contend that Israel, while being a Jewish state, protects the rights of non-Jews and secular Jews living within its borders. The Forum for National Responsibility is a group of prominent Israeli intellectuals, artists, and political leaders whose goal is to unite the people of Israel behind basic principles. The following document is known as "The Kinneret Agreement" and represented the group's vision for Israel's future.

As you read, consider the following questions:
1. According to the authors, what role should religion play in Israel?
2. How do the authors believe minorities in Israel should be treated?
3. According to the authors, what is the path to Middle East peace?

Forum for National Responsibility, "The Kinneret Agreement," January 11, 2002.

For more than one thousand and eight hundred years, the Jewish People was without a home. In countless lands and historical circumstances, we experienced persecution. In the twentieth century, under conditions of exile, the Jewish people sustained an historic catastrophe such as no other people has known, the Holocaust.

We believe that it is out of supreme and existential necessity, and with complete moral justification, that the Jewish people should have a national home of its own, the State of Israel.

Throughout its history, the Jewish people maintained a profound and unbroken connection to its land. The longing for the land of Israel and for Jerusalem stood at the center of its spiritual, cultural, and national life. The Jewish people's adherence to its heritage, its Torah, its language, and its land, is a human and historic occurrence with few parallels in the history of nations. It was this loyalty that gave rise to the Zionist movement [for a Jewish homeland], brought about the ingathering of our people once more into its land, and led to the founding of the State of Israel and the establishment of Jerusalem as its capital.

We affirm that the right of the Jewish people to lead a life of sovereignty in the land of Israel is an enduring and unquestionable right. The State of Israel fulfills in the land of Israel the Jewish People's right to life, sovereignty, and freedom.

The State of Israel is the national home of the Jewish people, the sanctuary of its spirit, and the foundation-stone of its freedom.

The State of Israel Is a Democracy

In accordance with its Declaration of Independence, the State of Israel is founded on the principles of freedom, justice, and peace. The State of Israel is committed to full equality of rights for all its citizens, without distinction of religion, origin, or gender. The State of Israel is committed to freedom of religion and conscience, language, education, and culture.

In accordance with its Basic Laws and fundamental values, the State of Israel believes in the dignity of man and his freedom, and is committed to the defense of human rights and

31

civil rights. All men are created in God's image.

Every citizen of Israel, man or woman, is equal to all others. All citizens of Israel are free individuals.

The State of Israel is a democracy, accepting the decisions of the majority, and honoring the rights of the minority. All citizens of Israel are full and equal partners in determining its character and its direction.

The State of Israel Is a Jewish State

Inasmuch as it is a Jewish state, Israel is the fulfillment of the right of the Jewish people to self-determination. By force of its values, the State of Israel is committed to the continuity of the Jewish people and its right to an independent life in its own sovereign state.

The Jewish character of Israel is expressed in a profound commitment to Jewish history and Jewish culture; in the state's connection to the Jews of the Diaspora, the Law of Return, and its efforts to encourage Aliya and absorption; in the Hebrew language, the principal language of the state, and the unique language of a unique Israeli creativity; in the festivals and official days of rest of the state, its symbols, and its anthem; in Hebrew culture with its Jewish roots, and in the state institutions devoted to its advancement; and in the Jewish educational system, whose purpose is to inculcate, along with general and scientific knowledge and the values of humanity, and along with loyalty to the state and love of the land of Israel and its vistas, the students' attachment to the Jewish people, the Jewish heritage, and the book of books.

The State of Israel has an existential interest in strengthening the Jewish Diaspora and deepening its relations with it. The State of Israel will assist Jewish education in all places in the world, and will come to the aid of Jews suffering distress for their Jewishness. The Jews of Israel and the Jews of the Diaspora are responsible for one another's welfare.

The State of Israel Is a Jewish-Democratic State

By force of the historic right of the Jewish people, and in accordance with the resolutions of the United Nations, the State of Israel is a Jewish state. In accordance with the basic principles on which it was established, the State of Israel is a democracy. There is no contradiction between Israel's character as a Jewish state and its character as a democracy. The existence of a Jewish state does not contravene democratic values, nor does it in any way infringe on the principle of freedom or the principle of civil equality.

In order to guarantee the continuity of a Jewish-democratic Israel, it is imperative that a substantial Jewish majority continues to be maintained within the state. This majority will be maintained only by moral means.

It is incumbent upon the State of Israel to give expression to the sense of closeness felt by Jews towards the members of every other national or religious group that sees itself as a full partner in the upbuilding of the state and in its defense.

The State of Israel Respects the Rights of the Arab Minority

The State of Israel is obligated to treat all of its citizens equally and impartially.

In areas in which Israeli citizens who are not Jews suffer from injustice and neglect, vigorous and immediate action is called for in order to bring about the fulfillment of the principle of civil equality in practice.

Israel will ensure the right of the Arab minority to maintain its linguistic, cultural, and national identity.

Jewish history and Jewish tradition have taught us the terrible consequences of discrimination against minorities. Israel cannot ignore these lessons. The Jewish character of the State of Israel will not serve as an excuse for discrimination between one citizen and another.

The State of Israel Is Committed to the Pursuit of Peace

From the day of its birth, Israel has been subject to conflict and bloodshed. In all the years of its existence, it has had to live with struggle, grief, and loss. Nevertheless, in all these years of conflict, Israel did not lose its belief in peace, nor its hope of attaining peace.

With that, Israel reserves the right to defend itself. It is imperative that this right be safeguarded, and that Israel maintain the ability to defend itself on a permanent basis.

The State of Israel is aware of the tragic character of the conflict in which it is involved. Israel wishes to bring an end to the conflict and to assuage the suffering of all its victims. Israel extends a hand to its neighbors, and seeks to establish a lasting peace in the Middle East.

The Jewish Homeland

When it begrudgingly granted Jews the permission to rebuild their despoiled homeland, the international community was thus only recognizing the Jews' natural right to the land—recognizing that Jews have a right to self-determination and political autonomy in their national homeland, and that that homeland was Israel.

Ilana Mercer, *WorldNetDaily*, July 3, 2002.

Israel is prepared, therefore, to recognize the legitimate rights of the neighboring Palestinian people, on condition that it recognizes the legitimate rights of the Jewish people. Israel has no wish to rule over another people, but it insists that no people and no state try to bring about its destruction as a Jewish state. Israel sees the principle of self-determination and its expression within the framework of national states, as well as a readiness for compromise on the part of both sides, as the basis for the resolution of the conflict.

The State of Israel Is Home to Many Communities

In the State of Israel, the tribes of Israel have gathered from many lands, and, together with the inhabitants of the land, Jews and non-Jews, have created in it a society of many aspects.

Israel's human and cultural mosaic is rich and unique. Out of an appreciation for the contribution of the variety of different communities to the founding and establishment of the state, and out of respect for each distinct culture and for each individual, it is incumbent upon Israel to cultivate and preserve the palette of traditions that exists within it.

It is imperative that Israel preserve a common cultural core, on the one hand, and cultural and communal freedom, on the other. Israel must create a tolerant human environment that will allow each identity group to bring out the best within itself, and permit all of these groups to live together in harmony and mutual respect.

The State of Israel Is a State of Fraternal Solidarity

In keeping with the dreams of its founders, Israel aspires to build and maintain a society committed to the pursuit of justice. Nevertheless, the years since Israel's founding have seen the entrenchment of severe social distresses in the country. We believe that there is a vital need to renew the spirit of Israeli brotherhood on a basis of equality of opportunity and social justice. Israel must heal the internal schisms that divide it and create a true partnership among its citizens. Israel must be a state of mutual responsibility.

It is imperative that the State of Israel be a moral society, sensitive to the hopes of the individuals and the communities within it. Ours must be a society that offers all its citizens a sense of partnership. Every individual in Israel deserves to have the opportunity to develop the abilities and potentialities within him. The allocation of public resources should afford every citizen the maximal possibilities to develop his talents and improve his life, without respect to his place of residence, origin, or gender. To achieve this, it is imperative that Israel invest more intensively in education and infrastructure in the communities of its periphery. Israel must be a country in which one can pursue the good life.

The State of Israel and the Jewish Religion

Israel is home to secular, traditional, and religious Jews. The growing alienation of these groups from one another is dangerous and destructive. We, secular, traditional, and religious Jews, each recognize the contribution of the others to the physical and spiritual existence of the Jewish people. We believe that the Jewish tradition has an important place in the public sphere and in the public aspects of the life of the state, but that the state must not impose religious norms on the private life of the individual. Disagreements over matters of religion and state should be resolved through discussion, without insult and incitement, by legal and democratic means, and out of a respect for one's neighbor.

We are one people. We share one past and one destiny. Despite disagreements and differences of worldview among us, all of us are committed to the continuity of Jewish life, to the continuity of the Jewish people, and to vouchsafing the future of the State of Israel.

National Responsibility

In establishing the State of Israel, the founders of the state performed an extraordinary historic deed. This deed has not ended; it is at its height. The return to Zion and the effort to found a Jewish-democratic sovereignty in the land of Israel stand, in the 21st century, before great challenges.

We, who have joined together in this agreement, see ourselves as responsible for carrying on this deed. We see the State of Israel as our shared home. In accepting upon ourselves this agreement, we pledge to undertake all that can and must be done to guarantee the existence, strength, and moral character of this home.

| "To have a state created expressly for one people constantly eats away and mocks the democratic-emancipatory aspects of Zionism."

Israel Should Not Remain a Jewish State

Joel Kovel

In the following viewpoint, Joel Kovel argues that Zionism— the movement to establish a Jewish homeland in Palestine— is inherently racist and imperialistic, which makes it incompatible with democracy. He states that there cannot be a democracy for just one people. The only way peace can be achieved in Palestine is for Israel to abandon Zionism, he claims. Joel Kovel is the author of *The Enemy of Nature* and teaches at Bard College in Annandale-on-Hudson.

As you read, consider the following questions:
1. According to the author, what negative aspects of the West did Israel's founders adopt?
2. Why does the author believe that Israel is not a democracy?
3. What role does the author believe anti-Semitism plays in the debate about Israel?

The Zionists took from the West the values of liberal democracy, but also the goals, tactics, and mentality of imperialism that often accompanied these. The convergence between tribalism and imperialism seemed, on the surface, to be a successful alignment of the various impulses of the Zionist project [to establish a Jewish homeland in Palestine]. From the first Jewish settlements in Palestine an imperialist mentality enabled Zionists to readily rationalize their displacement of indigenous Palestinians under the notion of a civilizing mission, embroidered with a full repertoire of Orientalist prejudices.

Zionism's allegiance to modernity also gave Zionism a high degree of technological prowess and organizational ability. During the years of the Yishuv, or settlement, this was evidenced by the degree to which Zionists would consistently out-produce and out-perform the indigenous peoples despite the great numerical superiority of the latter. Later, in the period of the wars leading up to the state of Israel, as well as the wars carried out by this state, superior organizational ability combined with superior weaponry made Israel into a regional juggernaut—one, moreover, driven by the talion law of tribalism and the racist reduction of one's adversary.

It was for some time easy to sympathize with a Jewish state and to overlook its imperialist tendencies, especially in the crucial period of the mid- to late 1940s, when evidence of the Holocaust surfaced as a diabolic reminder of Jewish vulnerability to the malignancies of so-called Western Civilization. I remember well as a youth of twelve the rush of joy and hope as it became increasingly clear that we were at last going to have "our state," and I know full well how deeply the Jews around me shared that feeling.

The Impossibility of a Promised Land

But neither understanding nor sympathy can nullify the judgment that in proceeding down this path, Zionism set the stage . . . for the present hellish outcome. And this has a great deal to do with the fact that the notion of a democratic Jewish state, despite its allure, is a logical impossibility and a trap. It is remarkable that so sophisticated a people should have so much trouble grasping the impossibility inherent in their notion of a Promised Land: a democracy that is only to be for a certain people cannot exist, for the elementary reason that the modern democratic state is defined by its claims of universality.

Modern nation-states are uneasy syntheses of the two terms: the nation, which embodies the lived, sensuous, territorial, and mythologized history of a people; and the state, which is the superordinate agency regulating a society and having the capacity, as Max Weber put it, to wield legitimate violence. In its pre-modern, non-democratic form, the nation-state could embrace directly the will of a particular national body. Under these circumstances, state power was held by those who controlled the nation. In practice, these were a mixture of kings and aristocrats who exerted direct territorial dominion, along with the theocrats of the priest class who controlled symbolic and mythopoetic production. Between the divine right of kings and the territorial powers of priests, the legality of pre-modern states took shape.

The democratic nation-state was a mutation of this arrangement, forged to accommodate the power of the newly emerging capitalist classes, but also to advance the notion of a universal human right—the stirring ideal that all human beings are created equally free before the law. The subsequent history of this political formation reveals, in all its fragility, the tensions inherent in the fitful development of human rights. But there should be no mistaking that our hopes for a world beyond tribalist revenge and the arbitrary power of rulers depend on strengthening and advancing the notion of universal human rights. The legitimacy of modern nation-states—the legitimacy of justice itself—rests upon this right. Of course, not all democratic nation-states are just in practice, nor have they necessarily come into being in ways consonant with the universal human rights they assert. The United States, Canada, Australia, and South Africa are just a few of the many examples of democratic nation-states that have come into existence through violence. The various horrors that have marked the history of these countries, however, have not prevented them from offering full participation in the polity to those who had been enslaved, expelled, and/or exterminated as the nation-state came into existence. Thus Ben Nighthorse Campbell, an American Indian, sits in the U.S. Senate, while Colin Powell and Condoleezza Rice, descendents of enslaved Africans, run U.S. foreign policy (needless to add, very cordially to Israel), and may someday be president.

A Racist Social Contract

None of this denies the racism that blocks the modern democratic state from keeping its promise. But there is a big difference between a state that fails to live up to its social contract because of a history saturated with racism, and one where the contract itself generates racism, as has been the case for a settler-colonial Israel which claims to be both a democracy and an ethnocracy organized by and for the Jewish people. Under such circumstances, racism is not an historical atavism, but an entirely normal, and constantly growing, feature of the political landscape. To have a state created expressly for one people constantly eats away and mocks the democratic-emancipatory aspects of Zionism. Zionism, in short, is built on an impossibility, and to live in it and be of it is to live a lie.

Not a Real Democracy

Israel, of course, not only is not a genuine democracy for its Arab citizens, and is something quite different for those who live under Israeli occupation, but is hardly a Western-style democracy for its Jewish citizens either. Reform and Conservative rabbis are not able to perform weddings and funerals, which are an Orthodox monopoly. Non-Orthodox Israelis serve in the army and pay university tuition. The Orthodox are exempt and receive free yeshiva studies. Public transport is banned for all Israelis on the Sabbath.

Allan C. Brownfeld, *Washington Report on Middle East Affairs*, April 2003.

In other instances of post settler-colonial states, the democratic promise, however compromised, confers legitimacy. In the case of Israel, the logic of the ethnocratic state rules out an authentic democracy and denies legitimacy. All the propaganda about Israel being the "only democracy in the Middle East" and so forth, is false at its core, no matter how many fine institutions are built there, or how many crumbs are thrown to the Arabs who are allowed to live within its bounds. This can be shown any number of ways, none more telling than the inability of Israel to write a Constitution with a Bill of Rights.

As we well know, there are many states in the modern world that proclaim themselves for a given people and are in many respects more unpleasant places than Israel, including some of the Islamic states, such as Pakistan or Saudi Arabia. But none of these assert extravagant claims for embodying the benefits of democratic modernity as does Israel. Thus one expects nothing from Pakistan or Saudi Arabia in the way of democratic right, and gets it; whereas Israel groans under the contradictions imposed by incorporating features of Western liberal democracy within a fundamentally premodern, tribalist mission.

A Split Psyche

In Israel, Jewish exceptionalism becomes the catalyst of a terrible splitting of the moral faculties, and, by extension, of the whole moral universe that polarizes Zionist thought. For God's chosen people, with their hard-earned identity of high-mindedness, by definition cannot sink into racist violence. "It can't be us," says the Zionist, when in fact it is precisely Zionists who are doing these things. The inevitable result becomes a splitting of the psyche that drives responsibility for one's acts out of the picture. Subjectively this means that the various faculties of conscience, desire, and agency dis-integrate and undergo separate paths of development. As a result, Zionism experiences no internal dialectic, no possibilities of correction, beneath its facade of exceptionalist virtue. The Covenant becomes a license giving the right to dominate instead of an obligation to moral development. Zionism therefore cannot grow; it can only repeat its crimes and degenerate further. Only a people that aspires to be so high can fall so low.

We may sum these effects as the presence of a "bad conscience" within Zionism. Here, badness refers to the effects of hatred, which is the primary affect that grows out of the splitting between the exalted standards of divine promise and the imperatives of tribalism and imperialism. A phe-

41

nomenally thin skin and denial of responsibility are the inevitable results. The inability to regard Palestinians as full human beings with equivalent human rights pricks the conscience, but the pain is turned on its head and pours out as hatred against those who would remind of betrayal: the Palestinians themselves and those others, especially Jews, who would call attention to Zionism's contradictions. Unable to tolerate criticism, the bad conscience immediately turns denial into projection. "It can't be us," becomes "it must be them," and this only worsens racism, violence, and the severity of the double standard. Thus the "self-hating Jew" is a mirror-image of a Zionism that cannot recognize itself. It is the screen upon which bad conscience can be projected. It is a guilt that cannot be transcended to become conscientiousness or real atonement, and which returns as persecutory accusation and renewed aggression.

The bad conscience of Zionism cannot distinguish between authentic criticism and the mirrored delusions of anti-Semitism lying ready-made in the swamps of our civilization and awakened by the current crisis. Both are threats, though the progressive critique is more telling, as it contests the concrete reality of Israel and points toward self-transformation by differentiating Jewishness from Zionism; while anti-Semitism regards the Jew abstractly and in a demonic form, as "Jewish money" or "Jewish conspiracies," and misses the real mark. Indeed, Zionism makes instrumental use of anti-Semitism, as a garbage pail into which all opposition can be thrown, and a germinator of fearfulness around which to rally Jews. This is not to discount the menace posed by anti-Semitism nor the need to struggle vigorously against it. But the greater need is to develop a genuinely critical perspective, and not be bullied into confusing critique of Israel with anti-Semitism. One cannot in conscience condemn anti-Semitism by rallying around Israel, when it is Israel that needs to be fundamentally changed if the world is to awaken from this nightmare.

Zionism Is the Problem

This is not the place to explore what such change would look like. But the guiding principle can be fairly directly stated. By forming Israel as a refuge and homeland for Jews from enturies of persecution, and especially by making the Faustan bargain with imperialism, those Jews who opted for Zionism negated their past sufferings, and turned their weakness into strength. But such strength, grounded in the domination, oppression, and expulsion of others, is worthless. Zionism negated what had been done to the Jews but failed to negate the negation itself, and thereby repeated the past with a different set of masks. If one doubts this, look at the set of oppressions forced upon Jews by Christendom—being forced into ghettos, denied ordinary rights such as land-holding, kicked around, massacred, expelled, and subjected to a racist system by the oppressors—and ask yourself whether the same have not been imposed upon Palestinians by the Zionist, with the only distinction worth noting being the terms of the racism?

It is never too late to remedy this state, and a sizable minority of people of good will are already moving in this direction, against great odds. But it would be irresponsible to gloss over the grim finding that the journey is conditioned by the fact that the core of the problem lies in Zionism itself, with its assumption that there can be a democratic state for one particular people. So long as this notion is held, poisonous contradictions will continue to spill forth from the ancient land variously called Palestine or Israel. And as a frankly non-democratic, or even fascist, Israel can scarcely be imagined as an improvement, we are led to the sober conclusion that a basic rethinking of Jewish exceptionalism must be the ground of any lasting or just peace in the region. The implications are many, and need to be worked out. But the time has come for the Jewish people to resume their striving toward universality.

> *"What if there were no place in the world
> today for a Jewish state? What if the
> binational solution were not just
> increasingly likely but actually desirable?"*

Israel Should Be a Binational State

Tony Judt

According to Tony Judt in the following viewpoint, by the time of Israel's creation in 1948, the world had begun to move toward inclusive societies that embrace multiple ethnicities, making Israel—a Jewish state—an anachronism since its founding. Judt argues that Israel must abandon its partiality toward Jews and embrace Palestinians as well, thereby forming a binational state. Tony Judt is a professor of history and director of the Remarque Institute at New York University.

As you read, consider the following questions:
1. According to Judt, what solution do right-wing Israelis have in mind for the Israeli-Palestinian conflict?
2. According to the author, what is the cause of the rise in attacks on Jews in Europe?
3. Why does the author believe the two-state solution is doomed?

will leave voluntarily, but no one believes it. Some will die and kill rather than move.

The time has come to think the unthinkable. The two-state solution—the core of the Oslo process and the road map—is probably already doomed. With every passing year we are postponing an inevitable, harder choice that only the far right and far left have acknowledged. Today, the Middle East peace process is finished. It did not die: It was killed. And the true alternative facing the region is between an ethnically cleansed Greater Israel and a single, integrated, binational state of Jews and Arabs, Israelis and Palestinians.

What if there were no place in the world today for a Jewish state? What if the binational solution were not just increasingly likely but actually desirable? It is not such a very odd thought.

An Oddity Among Democracies

Most of the readers of this essay live in pluralist states that have long since become multiethnic and multicultural. Israel itself is a multicultural society in all but name; yet it remains distinctive among democratic states in its resort to ethno-religious criteria with which to denominate and rank its citizens. It is an oddity among modern nations not because it is a Jewish state and no one wants the Jews to have a state, but because it is a Jewish state in which one community—Jews—is set above others, in an age when that sort of state has no place.

For many years, Israel had a special meaning for Jews. After 1948, it took in hundreds of thousands of helpless survivors with nowhere to go. Israel needed Jews and Jews needed Israel. The circumstances of its birth have thus bound Israel's identity inextricably to the Shoah, the German project to exterminate the Jews. As a result, all criticism of Israel is drawn ineluctably back to the memory of that project. To find fault with Israel is to think ill of Jews. To imagine an alternative configuration in the Middle East is to indulge the moral equivalent of genocide.

But today, non-Israeli Jews feel themselves once again exposed to criticism and vulnerable for things they didn't do. But this time it is a Jewish state, not a Christian one, holding them hostage. Diaspora Jews are implicitly identified with Israeli policies. The increased incidence of attacks on Jews in Europe and elsewhere is primarily attributable to misdirected efforts, often by young Muslims, to get back at Israel.

A Dysfunctional Anachronism

In a world where nations and peoples increasingly intermingle and intermarry, where cultural and national impediments to communication have all but collapsed, where more and more of us have multiple elective identities and would feel constrained if we had to answer to just one, in such a world, Israel is truly an anachronism. And not just an anachronism, but a dysfunctional one. In today's "clash of cultures" between open, pluralist democracies and belligerently intolerant, faith-driven ethno-states, Israel actually risks falling into the wrong camp.

"The fanatical hatred of Jews and all things Jewish aroused in the Palestinians . . . make any hope of a pluralist binational state . . . unthinkable."

Israel Should Not Be a Binational State

Jonathan Rosenblum

Europeans increasingly consider Israel to be a threat to world peace, according to Jonathan Rosenblum in the following viewpoint. Some have thus called for replacing the Jewish state with a binational one that would embrace both Jews and Palestinians, but this would never work, the author argues. Arabs would quickly take over Israel and oust the Jews, he claims. Jonathan Rosenblum is a columnist for the *Jerusalem Post.*

As you read, consider the following questions:
1. Why does the author believe many Europeans hate Israel?
2. How would a binational Israel resemble the former Yugoslavia, according to Rosenblum?
3. How do Europeans view nationalism, according to the author?

Jonathan Rosenblum, "Rush to Madness," *Hamodia*, November 7, 2003.

Despite the 1991 repeal of the U.N.'s [United Nation's] infamous "Zionism is racism" resolution, Israel's international standing is far worse today than it was in 1975 when the resolution was originally passed. The 1975 resolution drew almost all of its support from Arab countries and third-world dictatorships.

Today 60% of Europeans, according to a European Commission poll published [in November 2003], view Israel as the greatest threat to world peace. A greater threat than North Korea, whose entire economy is based on the export of nuclear weapons technology to anyone with the money to pay; a greater threat than Islamist terrorists, who are now deeply embedded in every Western nation.

Mainstream European statesmen and intellectuals deny Israel's legitimacy. The question posed by the *Guardian*—is the suffering of the Palestinians not too high a price for the humanitarian impulse to grant the Jews a state after the horrors of the Holocaust?—is now asked regularly in one European forum after another. "Israel no longer has a right to exist," leading British novelist A.N. Wilson announces without hestitation in the *Evening Standard* of London.

"I no longer feel comfortable in my own country," writes Melanie Phillips, one of Britain's best columnists, "because of the hatred that has welled up toward Israel and the Jews. . . . [A]t present it is open season on both Israel and Jews." The political Left in England has captured the intellectual establishment, writes Phillips, and promulgates the view that "Israel should not exist, that it is a Nazi state and that Jews control America."

Hatred of Israel

There are many reasons for the hatred of Israel in Europe. Europeans live in fear: fear of Arab oil power and fear of growing populations of increasingly alienated and radical Moslem populations in their midst, whom they hope to placate with condemnations of Israel. To these fears must be added guilt over Europe's colonial past and the cult of victimhood that justifies all violence by those identified as history's oppressed. These factors have led to a reemergence in polite society of an anti-Semitism not openly expressed since the Holocaust.

In this noxious brew, one more factor has received too little attention: the devaluation of the nation-state in modern European eyes. Europeans today tend to identify nationalism with the two world wars that claimed millions of lives in the century just past. As a consequence, ever more attributes of sovereignty are being transferred from European states to various European bureaucracies.

Zionism, of course, is an outgrowth of 19th century European nationalism. The solution to the "Jewish problem"—i.e., the suffering of stateless Jews at the hands of Europeans deeply rooted in their own nations—propounded by Zionism was the creation of a Jewish nation-state on the model of existing European states.

The pride that most Jews in Israel, and many around the globe, continue to feel in the creation of Israel, as well as the constant violence that has attended Israel since its birth make Israel the exemplar of a nationalism now discredited in European eyes. Europeans tend to forget that their own nations were each the product of a long series of conquests and wars in the course of which a linguistic and ethnic identity was fashioned. But that process took place in the nether regions of history. The return of the Jewish people to their land, by contrast, took place within living memory, and the constant war over Israel creation continues to this day.

The ultimate irony, writes University of Chicago professor Mark Lilla in the June 23 [2003] *New Republic*, is that "once upon a time, the Jews were mocked for not having a nation-state. Now they are criticized for having one."

Dismissal of Israel

Typical of that European attitude was Professor Tony Judt's dismissal of Israel, in the September 25 [2003] *New York Review of Books*, as "an anachronism." (Judt's terminology recalled the historian Arnold Toynbee's similar dismissal of the Jewish people as a historical atavism.) "The very idea of a 'Jewish state'—a state in which Jews and Jewish religion have exclusive privileges from which non-Jewish citizens are forever excluded—is rooted in another time and place," Judt concludes. In place of Israel, he calls for a binational state.

To make his case, Judt portrays Israel today as if the

Greater Israel ideology of settlers in Judea and Samaria, were regnant. Israel's leaders, as drawn by Judt, following Avraham Burg [speaker of the Israeli Knesset], are all fascists of exceptional malevolence.

The Destruction of Israel

A binational Israeli-Palestinian state—a dream of many peaceniks—is not politically viable even though it would be economically desirable. Jewish and Arab nationalism are realities; they cannot be wished away. Mutual hatred and suspicion are realities; they cannot be dismissed. Arguing against nationalism may work a hundred years from now but it doesn't fly today. A Jewish state—in which Jewish national culture is the dominant culture and most people speak Hebrew—is no more racist than would be an Arab state whose dominant culture and language reflected its people. Three million Palestinian refugees cannot return to the Jewish state without destroying the Jewish national character of the Jewish state.

Sherwin Wine, *Humanist*, September/October 2002.

That Judt himself is Jewish no longer occasions surprise. Indeed the discomfiture caused to Jews around the world by Israel is one of his reasons that it should cease to exist. Unkind things have been said to Judt at faculty dinner parties, and accordingly he would now like Israel to disappear.

What makes Judt's piece so frightening is that he is not a trendy professor of the far Left. He has written frequently for the ardently pro-Israel *New Republic*, and his major academic work sharply criticizes the infantile leftism of French intellectuals.

Despair at seeing any end to the Palestinian-Jewish conflict has driven Judt to propose mad solutions. For he surely knows that Jews would soon be demographically overwhelmed in the binational state he proposes, and few would wait around for that to take place before fleeing. His proposal is one not just for the end of Israel but for the end of Jewish settlement in the Land of Israel.

One State Is No Solution

While European nation-states may have generated most of the carnage of the first half of the 20th century, the greatest bloodlettings over the past half-century have been intramural affairs, usually in countries created by former colonial powers in which a multitude of ethnic groups were artificially forced together. Yugoslavia and Rwanda are the two most glaring examples. Iraq is potentially another. And a binational Jewish-Arab state, as any student of the British Mandate knows, would surely be one more.

One would suppose from Judt's proposal that the Jews of Israel find themselves opposed by exponents of the universal brotherhood of man. In point of fact, Jewish nationalism is opposed by a far more virulent and exclusivist Palestinian nationalism.

Apart from the Law of Return, which has its parallels in the constitutions of many European states, Jews enjoy no formal legal privileges in Israel denied to Arab citizens. By contrast, many Arab states explicitly deny Jews any rights of residence, and the Palestinians have repeatedly made it clear that they will not tolerate a Jewish presence in any Palestinian state that they might achieve.

A Binational State Is Unthinkable

The fanatical hatred of Jews and all things Jewish aroused in the Palestinians over the life of Oslo [Accords between Israel and the Palestinian Authority] make any hope of a pluralist binational state, like Judt's native Belgium, unthinkable. In addition, the contrasting political development of Jews and Palestinians makes the two groups incompatible in one state. Israel has produced a fully developed democracy, while the primary allegiances of Palestinians remain ones of clan. No Arab state has produced even an embryonic democracy, and there is no reason to think the Palestinians are well suited to be the first.

Judt himself knows that the binational state he proposes would be entirely dysfunctional. As Professor Lilla observes, "The European fantasy of the future Middle East is not of decent, liberal nation-states living side by side in peace, but of some sort of post-national, post-political order growing up under permanent international supervision. Not [former Jewish prime minister] Menachem Begin and [former Egyptian president] Anwar Sadat shaking hands, but [U.N.

weapons inspector] Hans Blix zipping around Palestine in his little truck."

And indeed that is precisely what Judt envisions: the security of Jews and Arabs permanently guaranteed by an international force and the emergence of a new political class among Jews and Arabs alike.

Alas, not a beautiful dream, but a recipe for a nightmare.

Periodical Bibliography

The following articles have been selected to supplement the diverse views presented in this chapter.

Barbara Amiel — "The Jewish Question: After an Exhausting 53 Years of War, the Question Is: Would It Really Matter if Israel Ceased to Exist as a Jewish State?" *Maclean's*, February 26, 2001.

Uri Avnery — "A Jewish Demographic State," *Washington Report on Middle East Affairs*, December 2002.

Abbie Bakan — "Opposing Colonialism in the Middle East: What's Left? A Rejoinder to Petras and Herman," *Canadian Dimension*, May/June 2002.

Azmi Bishara — "Apartheid Consciousness and the Palestine Question," *Canadian Dimension*, May 2001.

Allan C. Brownfeld — "Consensus Growing That, for Israel to Survive as a Jewish State, Occupation Must End," *Washington Report on Middle East Affairs*, March 2004.

Uri Dromi — "The Demographic Clock Is Ticking for Israel," *Israel Insider*, July 7, 2003.

Bernard Gilland — "Zionism, Israel, and the Arabs," *Contemporary Review*, January 2003.

Samah Jabr — "What Does Israel's 'Demographic Balancing Act' Hold in Store for Palestinians?" *Washington Report on Middle East Affairs*, March 2004.

Wallace Kantai — "Battling Israel to Keep as a Pure Jewish State?" *East African Standard*, June 6, 2004.

Ilana Mercer — "Israel Belongs to the Jews," *WorldNetDaily*, July 3, 2002. www.worldnetdaily.com.

Arthur Miller — "Why Israel Must Choose Justice: Without It, No State Can Endure as a Representative of the Jewish Nature," *Nation*, August 4, 2003.

Yakov M. Rabkin — "A Glimmer of Hope: A State of All Its Citizens," *Tikkun*, July/August 2002.

Hillel Schenker — "Israel's Dangerous Crossroads: A Continuation of the Current Situation Will Undermine Israeli Democracy," *Nation*, February 3, 2003.

Bret Stephens — "Eye on the Media: The Controversy of Israel," *Jerusalem Post*, October 31, 2003.

Mortimer B. Zuckerman — "Sheep, Wolves, and Reality," *U.S. News & World Report*, December 16, 2002.

CHAPTER 2

What Are the Roots of the Israeli-Palestinian Conflict?

Chapter Preface

The roots of the Arab-Israeli dispute, one of history's most intractable conflicts, can be traced back to the late nineteenth century, some sixty years before the modern state of Israel's founding. In 1896 Viennese journalist Theodor Herzl published *The Jewish State*, in which he called for the establishment of a Jewish nation in Palestine, the area in the Middle East that stretches from the Jordan River to the Mediterranean Sea. He convened the first World Zionist Congress in 1897 and helped to found Zionist organizations in other countries with large Jewish populations. Jewish immigration to Palestine, then controlled by the Ottoman Turks, increased. Zionism thus began as an international movement to establish a Jewish state in Palestine; after the founding of Israel, it evolved into a movement to support the Jewish state.

At the end of World War I, Palestine was placed under the administrative control of Great Britain in what was described as "the mandate." The mandate acknowledged the "historical connection of the Jewish people with Palestine" and instructed Britain to "facilitate Jewish immigration under suitable conditions." Over the complaints of the local Arab population, Jewish immigration to Palestine continued throughout the 1920s and 1930s, although Britain imposed numerical restrictions.

During World War II, widespread persecution led many European Jews to flee to Palestine. In response to the murder of 6 million Jews by the Nazis in World War II, in 1947 the United Nations voted by a two-thirds majority to divide Palestine into two states—one Jewish and one Palestinian. The UN plan proposed 53 percent of the land for a Jewish state and 47 percent for a Palestinian state. Jerusalem was to belong to neither side, instead being designated as an "international city." The Jews in Palestine eagerly accepted the partition because it would legitimize the Zionist goal; the Arabs, however, angrily rejected the partition because they opposed the creation of a Jewish state in Palestine. The following year, Israel declared its independence, and almost immediately, the first of five wars between Israel and its Arab neighbors broke out. It is illustrative of the deep divide between the two peoples that today, they cannot even agree on which party began these conflicts.

The intransigence of the conflict results from its underlying roots: battles over homeland and religion. Many Palestinians claim that Israel is a colonial occupying force, and that they were illegally driven from their ancestral lands. Many Israelis, however, believe that Zionism is the liberation movement of a persecuted people, and that their homeland in Israel is a birthright. These are powerful, emotional arguments. While there are voices of moderation and compromise among both Palestinians and Israelis, impartial observers agree that there has been little progress made toward a peaceful solution. The viewpoints in this chapter demonstrate that the convictions held by the opposing parties in the Arab-Israeli conflict sixty years ago are just as strong today. As a result, Israel's future remains as precarious today as it was on the day of its founding.

"Every time there is a dig in Israel, it does nothing but support the fact that Israelis have had a presence there for 3,000 years."

Israel Rightfully Belongs to the Jews

James Inhofe

James Inhofe is a Republican U.S. senator representing the state of Oklahoma. In the following viewpoint, which was originally given as a statement before the U.S. Senate on March 4, 2002, he argues that Israel's claim to its land predates the claims of other peoples. According to Inhofe, because Israel existed in Palestine up until the time of the Roman Empire, they have a right to the land today. Moreover, according to Inhofe, the Nazi Holocaust made the creation of a Jewish homeland a humanitarian necessity.

As you read, consider the following questions:
1. According to the author, who started the four wars between Israel and its Arab neighbors?
2. Why does the author believe that Israel is important to the United States?
3. According to the author, what is the biblical case for the existence of Israel?

James Inhofe, statement before the U.S. Senate, Washington, DC, March 4, 2002.

I was interested the other day when I heard that the de facto ruler, Saudi Arabian Crown Prince Abdullah, made a statement which was received by many in this country as if it were a statement of fact, as if it were something new, a concept for peace in the Middle East that no one had ever heard of before. I was kind of shocked that it was so well received by many people who had been down this road before.

I suggest to you that what Crown Prince Abdullah talked about a few days ago [March 2002] was not new at all. He talked about the fact that under the Abdullah plan, Arabs would normalize relations with Israel in exchange for the Jewish state surrendering the territory it received after the 1967 Six-Day War as if that were something new. He went on to talk about other land that had been acquired and had been taken by Israel.

I remember so well on December 4 [2001] when we covered all of this and the fact that there isn't anything new about the prospect of giving up land that is rightfully Israel's land in order to have peace.

When it gets right down to it, the land doesn't make that much difference because [Palestinian leader] Yasser Arafat and others don't recognize Israel's right to any of the land. They do not recognize Israel's right to exist.

I will discuss seven reasons, which I mentioned once before, why Israel is entitled to the land they have and that it should not be a part of the peace process.

If this is something that Israel wants to do, it is their business to do it. But anyone who has tried to put the pressure on Israel to do this is wrong.

We are going to be hit by skeptics who are going to say we will be attacked because of our support for Israel, and if we get out of the Middle East—that is us—all the problems will go away. That is just not true. If we withdraw, all of these problems will again come to our door.

I have some observations to make about that. But I would like to reemphasize once again the seven reasons that Israel has the right to their land. The first reason is that Israel has the right to the land because of all of the archeological evidence. That is reason, No. 1. All the archeological evidence supports it.

Every time there is a dig in Israel, it does nothing but support the fact that Israelis have had a presence there for 3,000 years. They have been there for a long time. The coins, the cities, the pottery, the culture—there are other people, groups that are there, but there is no mistaking the fact that Israelis have been present in that land for 3,000 years.

It predates any claims that other peoples in the regions may have. The ancient Philistines are extinct. Many other ancient peoples are extinct. They do not have the unbroken line to this date that the Israelis have.

Even the Egyptians of today are not racial Egyptians of 2,000, 3,000 years ago. They are primarily an Arab people. The land is called Egypt, but they are not the same racial and ethnic stock as the old Egyptians of the ancient world. The first Israelis are in fact descended from the original Israelites. The first proof, then, is the archeology.

The second proof of Israel's right to the land is the historic right. History supports it totally and completely. We know there has been an Israel up until the time of the Roman Empire. The Romans conquered the land. Israel had no homeland, although Jews were allowed to live there. They were driven from the land in two dispersions: One was in 70 A.D. and the other was in 135 A.D. But there was always a Jewish presence in the land.

The British and the Turks

The Turks, who took over about 700 years ago and ruled the land up until about World War I, had control. Then the land was conquered by the British. The Turks entered World War I on the side of Germany. The British knew they had to do something to punish Turkey, and also to break up that empire that was going to be a part of the whole effort of Germany in World War I. So the British sent troops against the Turks in the Holy Land.

One of the generals who was leading the British armies was a man named Allenby. Allenby was a Bible-believing Christian. He carried a Bible with him everywhere he went and he knew the significance of Jerusalem.

The night before the attack against Jerusalem to drive out the Turks, Allenby prayed that God would allow him to cap-

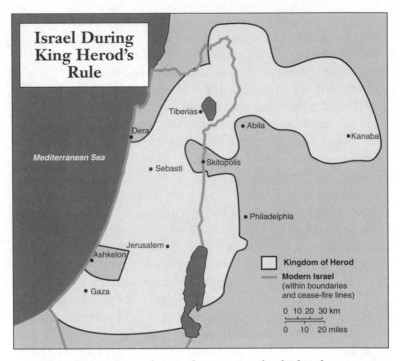

Israel During King Herod's Rule

Mediterranean Sea

Tiberias●
●Dera
●Abila
●Kanaba
● Sebasti
●Skitopolis
● Philadelphia
Jerusalem ●
Ashkelon
● Gaza

Kingdom of Herod
Modern Israel
(within boundaries
and cease-fire lines)

0 10 20 30 km

0   10   20 miles

ture the city without doing damage to the holy places.

That day, Allenby sent World War I biplanes over the city of Jerusalem to do a reconnaissance mission. You have to understand that the Turks had at that time never seen an airplane. So there they were, flying around. They looked in the sky and saw these fascinating inventions and did not know what they were, and they were terrified by them. Then they were told they were going to be opposed by a man named Allenby the next day, which means, in their language, "man sent from God" or "prophet from God." They dared not fight against a prophet from God, so the next morning, when Allenby went to take Jerusalem, he went in and captured it without firing a single shot.

The British Government was grateful to Jewish people around the world, particularly to one Jewish chemist who helped them manufacture niter. Niter is an ingredient that was used in nitroglycerin which was sent over from the New World. But they did not have a way of getting it to England. The German U-boats were shooting on the boats, so most of the niter they were trying to import to make nitroglycerin was at the bottom of the ocean. But a man named Weitzman, a Jewish chemist, discovered a way to make it from materials that existed in England. As a result, they were able to continue that supply.

The British at that time said they were going to give the Jewish people a homeland. That is all a part of history. It is all written down in history. They were gratified that the Jewish people, the bankers, came through and helped finance the war.

The homeland that Britain said it would set aside consisted of all of what is now Israel and all of what was then the nation of Jordan—the whole thing. That was what Britain promised to give the Jews in 1917.

In the beginning, there was some Arab support for this action. There was not a huge Arab population in the land at that time, and there is a reason for that. The land was not able to sustain a large population of people. It just did not have the development it needed to handle those people, and the land was not really wanted by anybody. Nobody really wanted this land. It was considered to be worthless land.

There Was No Palestinian Nation

I want the [Senate] to hear what Mark Twain said. And, of course, you may have read "Huckleberry Finn" and "Tom Sawyer." Mark Twain—Samuel Clemens—took a tour of Palestine in 1867. This is how he described that land. We are talking about Israel now. He said:

A desolate country whose soil is rich enough but is given over wholly to weeds. A silent, mournful expanse. We never saw a human being on the whole route. There was hardly a tree or a shrub anywhere. Even the olive and the cactus, those fast friends of a worthless soil, had almost deserted the country.

Where was this great Palestinian nation? It did not exist. It was not there. Palestinians were not there. Palestine was a region named by the Romans, but at that time it was under the control of Turkey, and there was no large mass of people there because the land would not support them.

This is the report that the Palestinian Royal Commission, created by the British, made. It quotes an account of the conditions on the coastal plain along the Mediterranean Sea in

1913. This is the Palestinian Royal Commission. They said:

> The road leading from Gaza to the north was only a summer track, suitable for transport by camels or carts. No orange groves, orchards or vineyards were to be seen until one reached the Yavnev village. Houses were mud. Schools did not exist. The western part toward the sea was almost a desert. The villages in this area were few and thinly populated. Many villages were deserted by their inhabitants.

That was 1913.

The French author Voltaire described Palestine as "a hopeless, dreary place."

In short, under the Turks the land suffered from neglect and low population. That is a historic fact. The nation became populated by both Jews and Arabs because the land came to prosper when Jews came back and began to reclaim it. Historically, they began to reclaim it. If there had never been any archeological evidence to support the rights of the Israelis to the territory, it is also important to recognize that other nations in the area have no long-standing claim to the country either.

Did you know that Saudi Arabia was not created until 1913, Lebanon until 1920? Iraq did not exist as a nation until 1932, Syria until 1941; the borders of Jordan were established in 1946 and Kuwait in 1961. Any of these nations that would say Israel is only a recent arrival would have to deny their own rights as recent arrivals as well. They did not exist as countries. They were all under the control of the Turks.

Historically, Israel gained its independence in 1948.

The third reason that land belongs to Israel is the practical value of the Israelis being there. Israel today is a modern marvel of agriculture. Israel is able to bring more food out of a desert environment than any other country in the world. The Arab nations ought to make Israel their friend and import technology from Israel that would allow all the Middle East, not just Israel, to become an exporter of food. Israel has unarguable success in its agriculture.

Humanitarian Reasons

The fourth reason I believe Israel has the right to the land is on the grounds of humanitarian concern. You see, there were

6 million Jews slaughtered in Europe in World War II. The persecution against the Jews had been very strong in Russia since the advent of communism. It was against them even before then under the Czars.

These people have a right to their homeland. If we are not going to allow them a homeland in the Middle East, then where? What other nation on Earth is going to cede territory, is going to give up land?

They are not asking for a great deal. The whole nation of Israel would fit into my home State of Oklahoma seven times. It would fit into the . . . State of Georgia seven times. They are not asking for a great deal. The whole nation of Israel is very small. It is a nation that, up until the time that claims started coming in, was not desired by anybody.

The fifth reason Israel ought to have their land is that she is a strategic ally of the United States. Whether we realize it or not, Israel is a detriment, an impediment, to certain groups hostile to democracies and hostile to what we believe in, hostile to that which makes us the greatest nation in the history of the world. They have kept them from taking complete control of the Middle East. If it were not for Israel, they would overrun the region. They are our strategic ally.

It is good to know we have a friend in the Middle East on whom we can count. They vote with us in the United Nations more than England, more than Canada, more than France, more than Germany—more than any other country in the world.

A Roadblock to Terrorism

The sixth reason is that Israel is a roadblock to terrorism. The war [on terror] we are now facing is not against a sovereign nation; it is against a group of terrorists who are very fluid, moving from one country to another. They are almost invisible. That is whom we are fighting against today.

We need every ally we can get. If we do not stop terrorism in the Middle East, it will be on our shores. We have said this again and again and again, and it is true.

One of the reasons I believe the spiritual door was opened for an attack against the United States of America is that the policy of our Government has been to ask the Israelis, and demand it with pressure, not to retaliate in a significant way against the terrorist strikes that have been launched against them.

Since its independence in 1948, Israel has fought four wars: The war in 1948 and 1949—that was the war for independence—the war in 1956, the Sinai campaign; the Six-Day War in 1967; and in 1973, the Yom Kippur War, the holiest day of the year, and that was with Egypt and Syria.

You have to understand that in all four cases, Israel was attacked. They were not the aggressor. Some people may argue that this was not true because they went in first in 1956, but they knew at that time that Egypt was building a huge military to become the aggressor. Israel, in fact, was not the aggressor and has not been the aggressor in any of the four wars.

Also, they won all four wars against impossible odds. They are great warriors. They consider a level playing field being outnumbered 2 to 1.

There were 39 Scud missiles that landed on Israeli soil during the gulf war. Our President [George H.W. Bush] asked Israel not to respond. In order to have the Arab nations on board, we asked Israel not to participate in the war. They showed tremendous restraint and did not. Now we have asked them to stand back and not do anything over these last several attacks.

We have criticized them. We have criticized them in our media. Local people in television and radio often criticize Israel, not knowing the true facts. We need to be informed.

I was so thrilled when I heard a reporter pose a question to our Secretary of State, Colin Powell. He said:

> Mr. Powell, the United States has advocated a policy of restraint in the Middle East. We have discouraged Israel from retaliation again and again and again because we've said it leads to continued escalation—that it escalates the violence. Are we going to follow that preaching ourselves?

Mr. Powell indicated we would strike back. In other words, we can tell Israel not to do it, but when it hits us, we are going to do something.

But all that changed in December [2002] when the Israelis went into the Gaza with gunships and into the West Bank with F-16s. With the exception of last May [2002], the Israelis had not used F-16s since the 1967 Six-Day War. And I am so proud of them because we have to stop terrorism. It is not going to go away. If Israel were driven into the sea tomorrow, if every Jew in the Middle East were killed, terrorism would not end. You know that in your heart. Terrorism would continue. It is not just a matter of Israel in the Middle East. It is the heart of the very people who are perpetrating this stuff. Should they be successful in overrunning Israel—which they won't be—but should they be, it would not be enough. They will never be satisfied.

Biblical Justification

No. 7, I believe very strongly that we ought to support Israel; that it has a right to the land. This is the most important reason: Because God said so. As I said a minute ago, look it up in the book of Genesis. It is right up there on the desk.

In Genesis 13:14–17, the Bible says:

> The Lord said to Abram, "Lift up now your eyes, and look from the place where you are northward, and southward, and eastward and westward. for all the land which you see, to you will I give it, and to your seed forever. . . . Arise, walk through the land in the length of it and in the breadth of it; for I will give it to thee."

That is God talking.

The Bible says that Abram removed his tent and came and dwelt in the plain of Mamre, which is in Hebron, and built there an altar before the Lord. Hebron is in the West Bank. It is at this place where God appeared to Abram and said, "I am giving you this land,"—the West Bank.

This is not a political battle at all. It is a contest over whether or not the word of God is true. The seven reasons, I am convinced, clearly establish that Israel has a right to the land.

[In 1994,] on the lawn of the White House, Yitzhak Rabin shook hands with PLO [Palestine Liberation Organization] Chairman Yasser Arafat. It was a historic occasion. It was a tragic occasion.

The Arabs Have Refused Peace

At that time, the official policy of the Government of Israel began to be, "Let us appease the terrorists. Let us begin to trade the land for peace." This process continued unabated up until last year [2002]. Here in our own Nation, at Camp David, in the summer of 2000, then Prime Minister of Israel Ehud Barak offered the most generous concessions to Yasser Arafat that had ever been laid on the table.

He offered him more than 90 percent of all the West Bank territory, sovereign control of it. There were some parts he did not want to offer, but in exchange for that he said he would give up land in Israel proper that the PLO had not even asked for.

And he also did the unthinkable. He even spoke of dividing Jerusalem and allowing the Palestinians to have their capital there in the East. Yasser Arafat stormed out of the meeting. Why did he storm out of the meeting? Everything he had said he wanted was offered there. It was put into his hands. Why did he storm out of the meeting?

A couple of months later, there began to be riots, terrorism. The riots began when now Prime Minister Ariel Sharon went to the Temple Mount. And this was used as the thing that lit the fire and that caused the explosion.

Did you know that Sharon did not go unannounced and that he contacted the Islamic authorities before he went and secured their permission and had permission to be there? It was no surprise.

The response was very carefully calculated. They knew the world would not pay attention to the details.

They would portray this in the Arab world as an attack upon the holy mosque. They would portray it as an attack upon that mosque and use it as an excuse to riot. Over the last 8 years, during this time of the peace process, where the Israeli public has pressured its leaders to give up land for peace because they are tired of fighting, there has been increased terror.

In fact, it has been greater in the last 8 years than any other time in Israel's history. Showing restraint and giving in has not produced any kind of peace. It is so much so that today the leftist peace movement in Israel does not exist because the people feel they were deceived.

They did offer a hand of peace, and it was not taken. That is why the politics of Israel have changed drastically over the past 12 months. The Israelis have come to see that, "No matter what we do, these people do not want to deal with us. . . . They want to destroy us." That is why even yet today the stationery of the PLO still has upon it the map of the entire state of Israel, not just the tiny little part they call the West Bank that they want. They want it all.

We have to get out of this mind-set that somehow you can buy peace in the Middle East by giving little plots of land. It has not worked before when it has been offered.

These seven reasons show why Israel is entitled to that land.

"Palestine is the land of prophets who were sent with the message of Islam and hence should not be ruled by anyone other than those who uphold the message of Islam."

Palestine Belongs to the Arabs

Islamic Assocation for Palestine

In the following viewpoint, the authors claim that the area known as Palestine is second in significance to Muslims only to Islam's holy cities of Mecca and Medina. The authors argue that Palestine was under Muslim control for most of history, with the exceptions of the time of the Crusades and the modern era beginning with the creation of Israel in 1948. The authors believe that the only solution to the violence that plagues the region is to return control of the land to Muslims. The Islamic Association for Palestine (IAP) is a not-for-profit national grassroots organization dedicated to advancing an Islamic solution to the Palestinian problem.

As you read, consider the following questions:
1. According to the authors, what is the importance of Palestine to Muslims?
2. Why do the authors believe Islamic rule will bring peace to Palestine?
3. According to the authors, what percentage of Palestine's population was Jewish at the time of British rule?

Islamic Association for Palestine, "The Islamic Cause of Palestine," www.iap.org, May 7, 2004. Copyright © 2004 by the Islamic Association for Palestine in North America. Reproduced by permission.

P alestine is a strategic land due to both its religious significance and geographic location. Throughout history it has been the center of the conflict and struggle between the Muslim World and Western Christendom. In the past century it has also become the center of the struggle between the Muslim World and the Jews. The significance of Palestine in the Islamic faith and throughout Islamic History is second only to the significance of Mecca and Madina. The loss of Palestine in 1948 is second only to the downfall of the Islamic Caliphate as the greatest loss to the Muslim Ummah [community] in this century, and the two events are strongly interlinked. What is the land of Palestine? What is its significance in Islam? What is the real nature of the conflict over Palestine? And what is the solution to its current occupation?

The Land of Palestine

Until the end of World War 1 Palestine was part of the Islamic Ottoman Empire. The Ottoman Empire stretched from North Africa to the Arabian Peninsula through the Fertile Crescent around the Black Sea and to the Adriatic Sea. The Ottoman Empire for centuries was the most tolerant state in the world and was a haven for the persecuted religious minorities of Europe especially, but not exclusively, the Jews. Such toleration was due to the fact that it based its laws and legislation on the [holy writings in the] Qur'an and Sunnah. Within the large Islamic state there were no clearly defined borders; however, the general area in which Palestine is now located was recognized as being part of Southern Belad al-Sham. After World War I, Palestine was separated from the general area that included what is known today as Syria, Jordan, and Lebanon by the British colonizers. For the first time in its history Palestine became a country with defined borders and a defined area estimated at 10,429 square miles. Its borders became: to the East the Jordan River, to the West the Mediterranean Sea, to the North Lebanon and to the South the Sinai Desert and the Gulf of Aqabah.

Palestine in Islamic Faith

The significance of Palestine in the Islamic faith is evident by the frequent references to it in both the Qur'an and the

71

Ahadith [sayings and traditions] of Prophet Muhammad. The greatest significance of Palestine for the Muslims is that it contains Baitul-Maqdis, the holiest place in Islam outside of the Hijaz. Both Al-Masjid Al-Aqsa and the Dome of the Rock are built in the area of the Baitul-Maqdis.

Baitul-Maqdis in Palestine was the center of Isra' and Mi'raj of Prophet Muhammad. In the Qur'an Allah says: "Glory be to the One who took his servant on a journey by night from Al-Masjid Al-Haram in Mecca to Al-Masjid Al-Aqsa whose precincts we have blessed. . . ." (Holy Qur'an, Surah Isra', Verse 1).

Baitul-Maqdis in Palestine was the second Mosque established on earth after Al-Masjid Al-Haram in Mecca. In the hadith Abu Dhar said: "Once I asked Prophet Muhammad what was the first mosque established on the earth; he said Al-Masjid Al-Haram. Then I asked him: then, which mosque? He replied: Al-Masjid Al-Aqsa. I then asked him what was the time period between the establishment of the two mosques; and he said: forty years."

Al-Bukhari Baitul-Maqdis in Palestine was the first Qibla (direction in which Muslims face when praying). The Muslims faced towards Baitul-Maqdis when praying during the entire Meccan period of Prophet Muhammad's life and for the first 16 months of the Medinian period, after which Allah ordered the Qibla to be changed towards the Kaaba in Mecca.

Muslims consider prayers in Al-Masjid Al-Aqsa to be equivalent to 500 times the prayers in any other mosque except for Al-Masjid Al-Haram in Mecca and Al-Masjid An-Nabawi in Madina. In the Hadith, Prophet Muhammad said: "Prayers in Al-Masjid Al-Haram are equivalent to 100,000 players, and prayers in my Masjid (in Madina) are equivalent to 1000 prayers, and prayers in Baitul-Maqdis are equivalent to 500 prayers."

In addition, there are several verses in the Holy Qur'an and several [in the] Ahadith of Prophet Muhammad that describe both the significance of Baitul-Maqdis in Islam and the fact that Allah has blessed the land around it. The various Qur'anic revelations and Prophetic statements concerning the blessed land of Palestine endeared the land to the companions (Sahaba) of Prophet Muhammad to such an extent that when Umar ibn Al-Khattab entered the region for the first time he announced that all the lands of Palestine would be part of the Islamic Waqf for the Muslim generations to come. After studying the various Qur'anic revelations, Prophetic traditions and practices of the companions to the Prophet, no rational mind could deny that Palestine as a blessed and holy land is of extreme importance and significance to every believer in Islam.

Palestine in Islamic History

The history of Palestine represents the history of Islam from the first prophet of Islam, Adam, to the last prophet of Islam, Muhammad. Palestine is the land of prophets who were sent with the message of Islam and hence should not be ruled by anyone other than those who uphold the message of Islam by implementing its laws and regulations.

Al-Masjid Al-Aqsa was the second mosque established on earth forty years after the establishment of Al-Masjid Al-Haram.

It is a holy site where many of the prophets were born or died, including Prophets Ibrahim, Lut, Dawood, Suleiman, Musa and Isa. While Dawood and Suleiman were able to create Islamic states in Palestine based on divinely ordained laws, according to both the Bible and the Qur'an, their descendants strayed from the path, transgressed against the laws revealed by God and thus brought upon themselves God's punishment, which included banishment from the holy land.

Baitul-Maqdis was the site of Isra' and Mi'raj of Prophet Muhammad during the Meccan period of his message.

Palestine was brought under Muslim control at the time of Umar ibn al-Khattab, the second Khalifa of the Muslims. Palestine was then made part of the Islamic state being ruled by Islamic law. The new laws were welcomed not only by the Muslims but also by the Jews and Christians of Palestine who had formerly been living under the tyrannical Byzantine yoke. The Byzantines were persecuting the Christians of the area because the Palestinian Christians belonged to a different Christian sect. The Muslims, however, guaranteed all Christians freedom of religion regardless of their sect.

73

In 1099 A.D. Palestine was invaded by the European Crusaders and subsequently occupied for nearly a century. During the occupation massacres and great injustices were committed against the Muslim, Jewish and native Christian residents of the area. The only law applied in the holy land blessed by God was the law of force and persecution.

In 1187 A.D. Palestine was liberated by the Muslims under the leadership of Salah al-Din Al-Ayyubi who brought back Islamic law to the area.

In 1916 the Arab elites announced their revolt against the Ottoman Islamic Empire at the instigation of the British who promised the Arabs an "Arab" rather than "Islamic" Kingdom.

In 1917 the British government issued the Balfour Declaration, which declared Palestine to be a homeland for Jews. At the time Jews made up approximately 8% of the population of Palestine and owned approximately 2.5% of the land.

A Crime Against Humanity

Palestine belongs to the Arabs in the same sense that England belongs to the English or France to the French. It is wrong and inhuman to impose the Jews on the Arabs. What is going on in Palestine today cannot be justified by any moral code of conduct. The mandates have no sanction but that of the last war. Surely it would be a crime against humanity to reduce the proud Arabs so that Palestine can be restored to the Jews partly or wholly as their national home.

Mohandas K. Gandhi, editorial in *Harijan*, November 11, 1938.

In 1918 the British and their Arab nationalist allies defeated the Ottomans. The British dismembered the Ottoman Empire and occupied Palestine. The British immediately began a campaign of immigrating European Jews to Palestine.

In 1948 the Jews claimed the establishment of a state for themselves over the land of Palestine and called it Israel. Hundreds of thousands of Muslims were forced out of Palestine under the military pressure of Jewish terrorist groups such as the Irgun, Levi, and Haganot, which were financed and armed by the British army.

In 1967 Israel attacked Egypt, Jordan and Syria, and occupied more land, including for the first time Al-Masjid Al-Aqsa. Since that time Al-Masjid Al-Aqsa has been the target of several attempts by the Jews to destroy or burn it, including several attempts to bring about its collapse through underground excavations. The Jews know that Al-Masjid Al-Aqsa is symbolic of the Islamic nature of the land and want to remove any trace of Islamic civilization from Palestine.

In December 1987, the Palestinians began an uprising (Intifada) in the West Bank and Gaza Strip against the continued Jewish occupation. The Intifada is still alive and strong in its 5th year. Despite thousands of deaths and injuries, the Palestinians are determined to maintain the struggle for their rights and dignity.

The Real Nature of the Conflict

When looking at the significance of Palestine within the Islamic faith and the central role it has played throughout Islamic history, the real nature of the conflict is a civilizational conflict waged between, on the one hand Islamic Civilization with its divinely inspired laws and mission to create on this earth the society of justice and freedom which has been ordained by God; and on the other hand, Western Civilization with its materialistic culture, worship of ethnicity and the state, and denial of God's supremacy. The existence of a Jewish state in the heart of the Muslim World and the occupation of Masjid Al-Aqsa is symbolic of the weakness of the Muslim Ummah and Muslims' own straying from the path of Islam in embracing imported ideologies. Masjid Al-Aqsa, Baitul-Maqdis, and the Blessed Lands of Palestine do not belong to the Palestinians or Arabs alone but to all Muslims, and only when the Muslims return to their faith and see the conflict in its real terms can they liberate Palestine as was done in the 12th Century by Salah al-Din Al-Ayyubi who, while not an Arab, knew his Islamic responsibility in undertaking the civilization struggle against the West and Islam.

Islam Is the Solution

Based on Palestine's Islamic history and significance in the Islamic faith, and after the failure of all non-Islamic methods to free Palestine from Zionist occupation, the Islamic solution is re-emerging as a powerful and popular means to liberate the occupied lands. Islam is a religion of peace secured by divine justice. Only Islam offers respect to all divinely revealed religions as it is the only religion which recognizes all the Prophets from Adam to Muhammad. It is the only religion which recognizes and believes that all the prophets brought the same essential message and thus all people deserve the freedom to worship as they please without persecution or harassment. For this reason, it has historically proven itself to be the only tolerant religion with regard to the peace and sanctity of the Holy Land. Only Islam can bring back peace to the Holy Land and security for the unrestricted and unharassed worship of God, the All-Mighty, by all who believe in Him whether Muslim, Christian, or Jew.

All Muslims, regardless of their ethnic background, nationality or language, are asked to join in freeing Palestine in the way Salah al-Din Al-Ayyubi, a Kurd, helped in the freeing of Palestine in an earlier era. As for their part, the Palestinian people have regained new strength in their rediscovery of Islam. As Muslims they prefer death and martyrdom, determined to fight for justice, be it only with stones. Forty-three years of occupation have brought neither peace nor stability to the Holy Land and history has proven that there can never be peace without justice. There will be no justice until all of the land is given back to its rightful owners who have been driven out of it. Any political plan which does not restore Palestine to its rightful owners, the Muslims, and any plan which does not bring back rule by Islamic law will not bring about real peace and will thus only lead to further violence, bloodshed, and instability.

"To this day, the state of Israel, which openly claims to be a state of Jews only, overtly and covertly discriminates against non-Jews."

The Racist Nature of Zionism Creates Conflict Between Israel and the Palestinians

Paul Eisen

In the following viewpoint, Paul Eisen argues that from its origins, the Zionist goal of displacing the non-Jewish population in Palestine and creating a Jewish state has been racist. He claims that the modern state of Israel, as the expression of that ideology, is therefore a racist state. He suggests that the only solution to the violence and misery in Palestine is the elimination of the ethnic nature of Israel. Paul Eisen is director of Deir Yassin Remembered, an organization whose purpose is to build a memorial to the Palestinian victims of the alleged April 9, 1948, massacre in Deir Yassin village.

As you read, consider the following questions:
1. How many native Palestinians does the author say were displaced in 1947 and 1948?
2. According to the author, what is Israel's plan for the occupied territories?
3. What is the "right of return"?

Political Zionism's aims were always clear—to establish, in all of Palestine, a Jewish state. There were exceptions of course, cultural Zionists who dreamed of a religious, cultural and spiritual home in Palestine alongside the indigenous population. But for the mainstream the objective, and the way to that objective, was clear—Palestine for Palestinians was to be transformed into Israel for Jews.

The strategy for achieving that objective was breathtaking. Above all, the Zionists knew how to wait. "The Negev will not run away," said Chaim Weitzman and, as he well knew, nor would the rest of Palestine. But wait for what? For what Ben-Gurion [Israel's first prime minister] called a "revolutionary situation," meaning a situation in which the takeover of Palestine could be completed. The first of these "revolutionary situations" presented itself in 1947 and 1948.

For Palestinians, like so many times before and after, the UN [United Nations] partitioning of their homeland was a no-win situation.[1] Like the Palestinian peasant farmer early in the [twentieth] century, confronted with settlers waving legal documents and demanding his eviction, Palestinians in 1947 simply could not win. If they resisted they lost their land, and if they didn't resist they also lost their land. In any event, Palestinian society was shattered by the Zionist onslaught; 750,000 Palestinians were expelled and 78 percent of historic Palestine became Israel.

Discrimination Against Non-Jews

Since then, Zionism, now institutionalized as the state of Israel, has continued its policy of discriminating against all non-Jews both within and outside its borders, and of ethnically cleansing Palestinians from Palestine. To this day, the state of Israel, which openly claims to be a state of Jews only, overtly and covertly discriminates against non-Jews.

So there's no nice way of saying it: Zionism is a discriminatory ideology, and Israel, the political expression of that ideology, is a discriminatory state. In any other situation, in any other time and place, and with any other people, both

---

1. The UN's plan to partition Palestine was intended to create a Jewish state and a Palestinian state.

would be termed racist. But not, it seems, when applied to here and now and to Israelis and Jews. So why is it that individuals and organizations who found it a simple enough matter to apply the label of racism to apartheid and South Africa find it virtually impossible to apply the same label to Zionism and Israel?

The answer is because white South Africans and Afrikaners are not Jews. White South Africans and Afrikaners have their own history of suffering, but this history has not been as protracted nor as intense as Jewish suffering, nor has it become so central to Western emotional and spiritual life. White South African and Afrikaner culture, religion and mythology, unlike Jewish culture, religion and mythology, have not provided the bedrock for much of Western culture, religion and mythology. And white South Africans and Afrikaners are not spread so widely, or so influentially, as Jews. It has also been argued that because of the particularities of Jewish history and suffering, Jews may do what no one else is allowed to do, meaning that, unlike anyone else, Jews are entitled to discriminate. It has therefore also been argued that even taking into account all the attendant injustices, the creation of a Jewish state was, at the time, necessary.

But all this is of little use to Palestinians, the victims of Zionism. Whether the world chooses to see Zionism and Israel as discriminatory, and whether we choose to label Zionism and Israel as racist, or even whether we decide that the creation of the state of Israel was a necessary evil, the suffering of Palestinians at the hands of Zionism and Israel remains undiminished.

There Is No "Occupation"

If 1948 was the first of Ben-Gurion's "revolutionary situations," another followed in 1967 when, under cover of the June War, Israel initiated the second phase of its conquest of Palestine. Since then the entire solidarity movement has united around the slogan "end the occupation."

This slogan, after over 35 years, so cosy and comfortable, seems like it has been with us forever and will be with us forever. To move on seems very dangerous indeed. For many, it has provided hope in an often hopeless situation. But this hope may be delusory since it can be argued that there is no "occupation" and there never was an occupation. If there were an occupation, and if the Israelis had ever the slightest intention of ending it, they would have done so years ago. The "occupation" is, in reality, the final stage in the 120 year-old Zionist conquest of Palestine.

So the slogan "end the occupation" could not only be a diversion from the real issues but also a smokescreen for the true intentions of the oppressor. Palestinians and their supporters can comfort themselves that by working to end the occupation, they are working towards justice, whilst Israelis and their supporters can comfort themselves that whilst everyone is busy ending the occupation, they can get on with the real business of conquering Palestine.

Legitimizing Ill-Gotten Gains

But many Jews and Israelis do want to end the occupation. For some, still committed Zionists, ending the occupation and fixing Israel's borders along 1967 lines, means legitimizing and securing the ill-gotten gains of 1948. For others, Jews of conscience, the slogan conceals a deep and abiding wish for the return of the beautiful Israel of their childhood. That Israel and Zionism never were beautiful, and never can be beautiful, is irrelevant.

"End the occupation," whether on banners and flyers, bellowed through loud hailers or repeated in a million e-mails has, so far, taken us nowhere. Surely something is wrong. Perhaps this something is that we're barking up the wrong tree—that it's not the occupation that's the problem, but the very nature of Israel itself, of which the occupation is a symptom.

Israel Must Reform

The road map is the latest stage in Zionism's eternal good cop/bad cop routine.[2] [Israeli prime minister] Sharon, the butcher, has softened up the victim. All he has to do is to sign and the pain will go away. Whether to sign or not is for Palestinians to decide, but before they do, they may note that the

2. a peace plan sponsored by the United States that calls for a Palestinian state

first condition of this road map is the need for the Palestinian Authority to reform itself. Well, perhaps it should, but what about Israel? Should not Israel also reform itself? Should we not now call on the state of Israel to begin a process of transforming itself from being an ethnic state for Jews to becoming a democratic state for all its citizens?

The UN's Anti-Zionist Resolution

The UN [United Nations] General Assembly based its 1975 anti-Zionist resolution on the UN's own definition of racial discrimination, adopted in 1965. According to the International Convention on the Elimination of All Forms of Racial Discrimination, racial discrimination is "any distinction, exclusion, restriction or preference based on race, colour, descent, or national or ethnic origin which has the purpose or effect of nullifying or impairing the recognition, enjoyment or exercise, on an equal footing, of human rights and fundamental freedoms in the political, economic, social, cultural or any other field of public life." As a definition of racism and racial discrimination, this statement is unassailable and, if one is honest about what Zionism is and what it signifies, the statement is an accurate definition of Zionism.

Kathleen and Bill Christison, *Counterpunch*, November 2003.

What's done is done and, to some degree, cannot be undone, but would not the pain of exile and dispossession be that much less if it were no longer justified by the legal acceptance of Israel's right to discriminate? Would not solutions to the problems caused by past injustice be more easily found if that injustice did not remain enshrined in law and custom?

And within Israel itself, would not the daily discriminations and humiliations endured by its own Palestinian citizens be much diminished if Israel was their state as well? And the agony of occupation, would it not be brought to an end that much more quickly and painlessly when the notion of a land for Jews only ceased to be recognized in law? And finally, the right of [Palestinians to] return which, as many of us are only now beginning to understand, and so many more of us need to understand, can neither be relinquished nor withheld: Would not the ending of Israel's ethnic basis provide new opportunities for generosity and compromise in the implementation of that sacred right? For those Jews and Israelis who claim to want peace and acceptance in the region, they must know that states that define themselves along ethnic lines are probably not states with which most Israelis, Jews or anyone else, would wish to associate themselves, and that this type of ethnic state is utterly unacceptable in the modern world.

The True Obstacle to Peace

Is not the ethnic basis of Israel a, if not the, major obstacle to the achievement of a just peace? Imagine how many more options would be open if there was not the insane need to maintain Israel's exclusive Jewish identity. Even with the terrible injustice of its establishment, a thriving Jewish community is now present in Palestine. There is a new nation in the Middle East. Now is the time, whilst acknowledging and rectifying the crimes of the past, to recognize the realities of the present and so move on to a new and just future. But can this take place whilst the basic injustice remains enshrined in the very being of the state of Israel?

Such a move could, but need not, preclude two states in Palestine. It could, but need not, preclude the name "Israel", and it certainly must not preclude the right of Israeli Jews to live where they are in peace and prosperity. Nor need it preclude, for the time being at least, a Jewish majority or a Jewish character, however defined. What it does, and must preclude are the rights and benefits of citizenship of that state being conferred on one ethnic group alone.

And the time to make this call is now, loud and clear. Not tucked away in obscure policy documents or vague statements about democracy throughout the region, and not only in articles and essays, but on banners, slogans and manifestos. Is it not now obvious to everyone that without such a development progress simply cannot be made? Let us say it now, loud and clear.

"Zionism is not racism, for the Jewish people is not a race."

Zionism Is Not Racist

Barry H. Block

Barry H. Block, a rabbi, serves on the boards of the American Jewish Society for Service and the Jewish Federation of San Antonio. In the following viewpoint, which was originally given as a sermon on October 26, 2001, he argues that the comparison of Israel to apartheid South Africa is anti-Semitic. According to Block, Zionism represents the Jewish dream of returning to their ancestral home and the creation of a Jewish state there. He states that Zionism is not racist because the Jewish people are not one race. He claims that Zionism is a liberation movement in response to the historical persecution of the Jewish people. Finally, he suggests that Israel, as the product of Zionism, cannot be racist because it is a democracy.

As you read, consider the following questions:
1. During World War II, why did many Jews immigrate to Palestine, according to the author?
2. How has the UN's view of Israel changed over the years?
3. According to the author, how did Jews and Arabs react to the 1947 UN vote to create both a Jewish and a Palestinian state?

When I was in sixth grade, I pulled my first "all nighter." A friend and I had embarked on a project to build a scale model of the United Nations. We procrastinated. We didn't start to build until the afternoon before the project was due. Making matters worse, I am not handy. My partner had to do most of the building. Working at my friend's house, we were sustained on chocolate and hot tea, and we literally didn't go to sleep until the United Nations complex was fully constructed at six o'clock in the morning. We delivered the project to school, and promptly went home to sleep all day.

In those days, almost all Americans took pride in the United Nations and in the role we believed it could play in maintaining world peace. That international organization held a special place in the hearts of Jews around the world, for it had paved the way for the establishment of the State of Israel. In 1947, the U.N. voted, by two thirds majority, to create two states, a Jewish State and an Arab State, side by side in Palestine.

That 1947 vote was an international endorsement of Zionism, the eternal hope of the Jewish people for the reestablishment of Jewish sovereignty in our ancient homeland. Twenty-eight years later, though, the same body, the General Assembly of the United Nations, took a very different stance. In 1975, only months after the proud completion of my sixth grade United Nations project, that organization declared Israel to be "the racist regime in occupied Palestine," and labeled Zionism as "a form of racialism and racial discrimination."

The truth be told, the resolution equating Zionism with racism had very little impact. In the 1990s, after Israeli Prime Minister Yitzhak Rabin and P.L.O. [Palestine Liberation Organization] Chairman Yasser Arafat signed their understanding on the White House lawn, the U.N. resolution on Zionism and racism was repealed.[1] Once again, the world seemed to endorse Zionism, or at least to accept it.

Then, last year [September 2001], the peace came to an

1. On September 13, 1993, Israel and the P.L.O. signed an agreement that transferred authority in the West Bank and Gaza Strip to the new Palestinian Authority.

arriage and divorce within their own communities. A[...] et, public housing for Arabs is not as commodious as pu[...] ic housing for Jews. Jewish schools are superior. Infrastru[...] ure, from roads to sewers, is better in Jewish areas.

In short, even before we embark on discussion of the O[...] cupied Territories, Israel has a long way to go in its treatme[...] of its non-Jewish citizens. And yet, Israel is a free countr[...] The inequalities that I describe are detailed in the Israe[...] press and examined by Israeli courts. They are debated by I[...] raeli society and managed openly by Israeli Cabinet Mir[...] istries. We, too, may join in the criticism. In June [2001], ou[...] Central Conference of American Rabbis passed a resolution[...] calling upon Israel to end these inequities, to improve the l[...] of its minority citizens. Zionism is not racism, but the Stat[...] of Israel, like every nation on Earth, could be better than it i[...]

Disagreements with the Israeli Government

We Reform Jews have a number of disagreements with the current Israeli government, and with its predecessors. Most emphatically, we have consistently opposed the addition and growth of Jewish settlements in the West Bank and Gaza Strip. We may question the intensity of Israeli military reprisals, even after the most heinous of Palestinian terror attacks. We urge the Israeli government to do everything in its power to return to the negotiating table, to bring peace to Jerusalem. In his column in this month's [October 2001] *Temple Bulletin*, Rabbi Stahl noted that we may indeed criticize Israel, but we do so "out of love and out of a commitment to its ongoing survival and its prosperity." We are Zionists. We love Israel. We support Israel. Because of that love and support, we want Israel to be better than it is.

Lest we forget, one more reason that Zionism is not racism must be emphasized: True Zionists support the eventual establishment of a Palestinian State. In 1947, when the United Nations voted to create Israel, it also voted to create an Arab State in Palestine, next to Israel. That vote represented a compromise. The Zionists accepted the solution. The Arabs declared war. In the summer of 2000, that two-state compromise was again offered by Israeli Prime Minister Barak, with the support of President [Bill] Clinton. Tragically, Chairman

end. Now, we hear the renewed charge that Zionism is racism. Some months ago [August/September 2001], in Durban, South Africa, the U.N. Conference on Racism was hijacked by forces seeking to use that forum as a platform against Israel. No other regime in the entire world was similarly targeted. Words against Israel were not balanced by condemnation of Palestinian terrorism. Saddam Hussein's Iraq was not mentioned. Not a negative word was spoken against the Taliban [the terrorist-supporting regime in Afghanistan].

Israel Is Not Like South Africa

Occasionally, we Jews imagine ourselves to be hated by the entire world. As the old saying goes, "Just because you're paranoid doesn't mean that you don't have real enemies." The Durban conference, and world events that have followed, remind us that Israel does have profound enemies. With the inestimably significant exception of the United States, much of the world is indeed prepared to focus on the misdeeds, both real and imagined, of the Jewish people, to the exclusion of all others. "Zionism," the world tells us, "is racism."

My friends, I do not stand before you tonight to declare that Zionism is not racism. Such a charge does not dignify a response. The very suggestion that Israel can be compared to apartheid South Africa is the worst kind of anti-Semitism, plain and simple.

At the same time, we may all benefit from a review of the reasons that Zionism is not racism. We may renew of our commitment to the true meaning and principles of Zionism.

Zionism is not racism, for the Jewish people is not a race. Yes, Judaism is passed from parents to child, from generation to generation . . . with the transmission of the Torah through four generations in our Bar Mitzvah celebrant's family. And yet, a convert to Judaism is every bit as Jewish as a person who is born into our faith. Our own congregation is blessed with hundreds of Jews-by-Choice, who enrich the fabric of our community and who faithfully observe our traditions. Converts swelled the ranks of the Jewish people some 2000 years ago, dramatically altering the composition and appearance of our Jewish family. Today, a slim majority of the children in our Temple Beth-El Religious School have two Jewish parents, while only a substantial minority have four Jewish grandparents. We have more than a few Jews of Latino heritage in our congregation, and Jews of African or Middle Eastern descent are widespread in the world today. The Jewish people do not constitute a race. Zionism is not racism.

Zionism Is a Liberation Movement

Zionism is not racism, because it is a liberation movement for the Jewish people. Ever since the year 70, when the Second Temple was destroyed and our people dispersed, religious Jews have prayed for return to Zion. And yet, in 19th-Century Europe, Jewish people achieved unprecedented freedom. For the first time ever, Jews could be citizens of the countries where they lived. Many stopped praying for return to the Promised Land, for they believed that they had found it in Europe or America.

What Zionism Means

Zionism is our attempt to build a society, imperfect though it may be, in which the visions of the prophets of Israel will be realized. I know that we have problems. I know that many disagree with our government's policies. Many in Israel too disagree from time to time with the government's policies and are free to do so because Zionism has created the first and only real democratic state in a part of the world that never really knew democracy and freedom of speech.

Chaim Herzog, speech to the United Nations, November 10, 1975.

Then, in the 1890s, anti-Semitism raised its ugly head in France, seemingly the most enlightened of modern European nations. Europe was not the Promised Land. Modern Zionism was conceived as a way that the Jewish people could live in the world on an equal footing with other peoples of the world. In Eastern Europe, where virulent anti-Semitism never abated, Zionism was viewed as an escape from the harsh persecutions of Poland and Russia. While many European and American Jews still scoffed at the idea in the early decades of the 20th Century, Zionism began to unite world Jewry as Hitler came to power.

Jews in Europe were murdered by the millions, for no

reason, save that they were Jews. If our people
cape, they had no place to go. The British con
tine, and they outlawed almost all Jewish immig
homeland. The United States and Canada in
immigration quotas. Our people were slaugh
Nazis, but also because the rest of the world t
ear to our pleas. On the other hand, Jews alrea
Palestine, Zionists, put their lives on the line to
periled European Jews into Palestine. Occasi
succeeded. More often, the British turned them
end of the Holocaust, millions of Jews had no
Thousands upon thousands of our people were r
ing for years in Concentration Camps, now calle
Persons Camps, operated by the victorious allies

The 19th Century proved to the world that
ment would not bring an end to anti-Semitism.
caust proved that our Jewish people could not be
world without a free and secure independent Je
No other nation on the world would guarantee t
of Judaism and the Jewish people. Only the Jewi
with a Jewish State, could accomplish that vital ta
ating and saving the life of one's own people is n
Zionism is not racism.

Israel Is a Democracy

Finally, Zionism is not racism, because Israel is a de
To be perfectly honest, the State of Israel was fou
paradox. On the one hand, it is a Jewish State. To
the unique Jewish character of Israel and to secure
vival of our people, Israel must maintain a solid Je
jority. On the other hand, all citizens of Israel have
to vote, be they Arab or Jew, Muslim or Christian o
By definition, Israeli Arabs are full citizens of Israe
same time, we must acknowledge that they are seco
citizens. Arab and Druze Israelis are not part of the g
whom and for whom the nation exists.

Israel constantly struggles to get this balance righ
sit in the Knesset, Israel's Parliament. They elect th
local authorities. Muslims, Christians, and Druze ha
own religious authorities with full autonomy in mat

Arafat declined. In the months since that day, Jewish support for a Palestinian state has eroded. And yet, tonight [October 2001], as in 1947, we ask, may the Jewish people pray for the realization of the national hopes and dreams of the Palestinian people. Today, so different from 1947, may the Palestinian people accept the compromise. May they agree to live in their own nation, at peace, alongside the Jewish people in the State of Israel.

Zionism is not racism, because ultimately, Zionism is a messianic dream. For centuries, the Jewish people believed that the return to Zion would come only with God's redemption in the coming of the Messiah. Then, in the last century, we took a first step to salvation: a State of Israel in a pre-Messianic world. We may yet dream of a world of perfect harmony. We may yet pray for a world without divisions of race or nation, color or creed. And yet, we do not live in that world. Until the Messianic Age arrives, Zionism is survival for the Jewish people. The State of Israel is not an option.

May the world soon know that Zionism is redemptive, as the Jewish people continues to find salvation in our ancestral homeland. Through the treatment of its Arab citizens, may Israel soon show the world that Zionism strives for a better future. May God find Israel pleasing, in the pursuit of peace, for Zionism is a beautiful dream.

Amen.

*"There is no such thing as a Palestinian
above suspicion."*

The Palestinians Are Terrorists

Jonathan Rosenblum

In the following viewpoint, Jonathan Rosenblum argues that
all Palestinians must be treated as potential terrorists who are
eager to kill Israeli Jews and eradicate Israel. He suggests that
it is absurd for America to encourage Palestinian Authority
chairman Yasir Arafat to control terrorism because Arafat is a
terrorist and has turned Palestinian society into a death cult.
According to Rosenblum, there is no hope of peace in the
Middle East until Palestinians are forced to abandon terrorism. Jonathan Rosenblum is a regular contributor to *Hamodia*,
a Jewish Orthodox weekly newspaper published in the United
States, the United Kingdom, and Israel.

As you read, consider the following questions:
1. According to the author, why are Israeli security
   checkpoints necessary?
2. Why does the author describe the Palestinians as being
   part of a death cult?
3. According to the author, what role do Muslim religious
   leaders play in the terrorist attacks in Israel?

"It is crucial [for Israel] to distinguish between terrorists and ordinary Palestinians seeking to provide for their families," President [George W.] Bush advised Israel in his April 4 [2002] Rose Garden address. "The Israeli government should be compassionate at checkpoints and border crossings, sparing innocent Palestinians daily humiliation."

Israel would be delighted to be able to distinguish between terrorists and innocents. Unfortunately, the President neglected to provide any advice on precisely how to make that distinction.

All Palestinians Are Suspects

There is no such thing as a Palestinian above suspicion. Last January [2002], Wafa Idris became the first Palestinian woman suicide bomber. Copycats were not long in coming. During Pesach, an 18-year-old Palestinian girl blew herself up in Jerusalem's Kiryat Yovel neighborhood. Last week [April 2002], Israeli security forces arrested a woman in Tulkarm (one day after the Israeli pullback from the city), who was planning to carry her deadly load into Israel disguised as a pregnant woman. Two days later, a 17-year-old Palestinian succeeded with the same ruse, smuggling a "baby" of ten kilograms of explosives into Jerusalem's Mahane Yehudah market, where she killed 6 and injured 65 more, six of them critically. It is now believed that the ambush in Jenin in which 13 Israeli soldiers lost their lives was triggered by a suicide bomber in his early teens at most.

Just as there are no people above suspicion, so are there no vehicles that don't need to be searched. Idris was ferried to Jerusalem in a Red Crescent ambulance. Recently an explosive belt was discovered underneath a six-year-old Palestinian ostensibly being taken to a hospital by a Palestinian ambulance.

Security checkpoints are an inevitable consequence of Israel's inability to tell which "innocent" Palestinian workman or woman is today's suicide bomber. And those checkpoints will inevitably be slow-moving, humiliating affairs, especially when every vehicle must be thoroughly searched and explosive belts can be transported under every type of clothing.

Every Jew in Israel Is a Target

The dichotomy drawn by the President between innocent Palestinians and terrorists will not bear scrutiny. This is not a conventional war between two armies, but something entirely new: a war between two populations. Almost every Palestinian is a potential suicide bomber and every Jew living in Israel a potential target.

Over the nine years since Oslo [the 1993 agreements between Israel and the PLO], [Palestinian leader Yasir] Arafat . . . whipped the Palestinian population into a frenzy of hatred. True, not every Palestinian is yet ready to strap an explosive belt to his or her body, but the overwhelming majority of the Palestinian population supports suicide bombings. Spontaneous celebrations invariably break out in Palestinian towns after every "successful" suicide bombing. Parents of suicide bombers rejoice in their offspring's heroic actions, and tell the eager Palestinian media of their hopes that their remaining children will follow a similar path.

Palestinian opinion polls consistently find support for suicide bombings against Jewish targets hovering around 75%. Let the United States take note, a November 2000 poll by Bir Zeit University researchers showed an equal level of support for suicide attacks on American targets. And the official Palestinian paper *Al Hayat* editorialized . . . that "Palestinian suicide bombers are the noble successors of . . . the Lebanese suicide bombers who taught the U.S. Marines a tough lesson [killing 241 in a suicide bombing of a Marine barracks in 1983]."

All the President's lectures to Arafat for not having done enough to stop terrorism presume that somehow Arafat is on one side and the terrorists on the other. That too is preposterous. Arafat is the father of modern terrorism, and has never renounced its use. The PLO [Palestine Liberation Organization] was formed in 1964, three years before Israel took possession of the West Bank and Gaza. In its first major action, the same year, a PLO guerrilla squad attempted to blow up an Israeli pumping station. The goal: to provoke an Israeli retaliation that would ignite a pan-Arab offensive against the Jewish state. Nearly forty years later, Arafat continues to pursue the same strategy. Only today suicide bombings are the trigger with which he seeks to ignite a full-scale war involving all the Arab states.

The Palestinian Death Cult

The Palestinian Authority media, which is fully controlled by Arafat, plays a major role in the creation of the Palestinian death cult. Moslem clergy appointed and supported by the Palestinian Authority regularly broadcast sermons on PA [Palestinian Authority] television extolling martyrdom as the highest goal of the faithful and suicide bombings as the highest form of martyrdom. Last Friday's [in April 2002] TV sermon proclaimed the belief "that one day we shall enter Jerusalem as conquerors, Jaffa as conquerors, Ramle and Lod . . . and all of Palestine as conquerors."

"Now the darn Israelis won't let us into their country to enjoy an honest day's work!"

Lurie. Copyright © 2003 by Cartoonews International Syndicate, NYC. Reproduced by permission.

The preacher then castigated "whoever has not merited martyrdom in these times," calling on them "to rise in the night and call out, 'My Lord, why have you denied me martyrdom.'" That reproach to all those who are not yet martyrs echoed Arafat's response to the Seder night massacre in Netanya (as quoted in the *Washington Post*), "Give me martyrdom like this."

Calendars and posters glorifying suicide bombers sprout after every attack. Documents found in Arafat's compound reveal that the Palestinian Authority pays directly for the publicity when the suicide bombers are members of the Al-Aksa Martyrs Brigade. Three days after Arafat condemned suicide bombings against Israeli civilians in a February 3 [2002] *New York Times* op-ed piece, his Fatah movement sponsored a demonstration of elementary school girls carrying posters of Wafa Idris, the first woman suicide bomber.

The Palestinian Authority's support for the terror apparatus goes far beyond mere moral support. IDF [Israeli Defence Force] commanders in Operation Defensive Shield [the April 2002 military incursion in the West Bank] confess to being amazed by the quantity and sophistication of the bomb-making laboratories uncovered. Such a vast terrorist network could not have been established and maintained without the active complicity of Arafat at every step.

Arafat Controls the Terrorists

The connection between Arafat and the terrorist infrastructure, however, is no longer just a matter of logical inference. In the past three months [since 2002 began], more than half of the suicide bombers were dispatched by groups under Arafat's direct authority: the Al-Aksa Martyrs Brigade and Fatah-Tanzim. Asked by the *New York Times'* Joel Brinkley whether Arafat had ever asked them to cease suicide bombings, Naser Badawi, a political leader of the Al-Aksa Martyrs Brigade, answered in the negative.

Israeli searches of Arafat's compound turned up the "smoking gun" linking the Palestinian Authority directly to the terrorist network. [Israeli] Prime Minister Sharon read in the Knesset . . . two requests for funding from leading terrorists on which Arafat had affixed his personal approval. A third document, which the Prime Minister did not read, is from the Tulkarm district commander of the PA's General Intelligence Service to a superior. The local commander sings the praises of a squad that succeeded in killing six Jews at a bat mitzvah party, and boasts of that squad's close cooperation with the Palestinian General Intelligence Service.

Arafat has not only enlisted nearly the entire Palestinian

population as active combatants or enthusiastic supporters of terror attacks on Israel, he has targeted every sector of the Jewish population, regardless of sex, age, and geography. Those attacks have been calculated with fiendish precision.

Women as Targets

Demography is one of the weapons upon which Palestinians rely for their ultimate victory, and they have therefore deliberately targeted Jewish mothers and children. Of Jewish motorists killed in drive-by shootings and by snipers, a disproportionate percentage have been women. The suicide bomber who plunged last month [March 2002] into a group of mothers pushing baby strollers, in Jerusalem's Beit Yisrael neighborhood, committed the ideal atrocity from the Palestinian point of view.

The large number of recent suicide attacks on restaurants and cafes in the heart of Israel's major cities have been designed to deprive the Jews of Israel of any semblance of a normal life or the enjoyment of leisure activities of any kind. The Chol HaMoed attacks on an Arab-run restaurant in Haifa and on a health care clinic in Efrat later the same day carried an additional message to Arabs and Jews alike: No attempt at peaceful coexistence will be tolerated by the Palestinian Authority.

The Efrat health clinic serves Arabs from surrounding villages, as well as the residents of Efrat. When Arabs from those villages recently told a camera crew from Russian-TV of their gratitude to Efrat for extending quality medical coverage to them, the Palestinian Authority could no longer tolerate the use of the health care center by Arabs.

Finally, the Seder night massacre, which left 27 Jews dead, was an expression of absolute contempt for everything Jewish.

Eliminating Jews from Palestine

Arafat is close to realizing his vision of a total war in which everybody is a combatant, whether willingly on the Palestinian side, or unwillingly on the Jewish side. His guiding vision has always been a Palestine free of all Jews. While the Jewish population of Eretz Yisrael has, in the main, long since accepted that they will have to coexist with a large Arab population, Arafat and his people view the future in much simpler terms: only one people will survive on this narrow strip of land.

Until the Palestinians are forced to renounce their belief in such an "it's us or them" resolution, there can be no hope of peace. President [George W.] Bush's failure to adequately address the core of the problem, and to focus instead on a distinction between "innocent" Palestinians and terrorists, which bears no relation to the realities on the ground, will not force them to do so.

"Israel must be declared a terrorist state."

Israel Is a Terrorist State

Patrick Johnston

In the following viewpoint, Patrick Johnston urges the UN General Assembly and Security Council to pass resolutions condemning Israel and branding it a terrorist state because of its human rights violations. He argues that Israel has no legal right to assassinate Palestinian Authority chairman Yasir Arafat, as it has expressed its intention to do. He also claims that because the United States provides material and moral support to Israel, it also is committing illegal actions and must be brought to justice. Patrick Johnston is a member of VoxRx.org, a UN Culture of Peace human rights nongovernmental organization.

As you read, consider the following questions:
1. According to the author, how does Israel use the media?
2. How does the author think Israeli prime minister Ariel Sharon should be treated?
3. Of what crimes related to Israel does the author believe the United States is guilty?

The United Nations General Assembly must pass resolutions declaring Israel to be in violation of the UN Charter of Member States and suspend Israel from the United Nations effective immediately. Further, both the General Assembly and the Security Council must pass resolutions imposing the harshest yet sanctions and complete international isolation against Israel for continued reckless and wanton violations of numerous resolutions concerning the criminal treatment of the Palestinian people and mandates on Palestine.

1. Israel must be declared a terrorist state
2. Zionism must be declared a terrorist movement and [its] followers terrorists
3. War crimes tribunals must be sought against appropriate Israeli leaders
4. UN must impose harsh sanctions and isolation against Israel

End U.S. Support for Israel

The United States must wake up to the fact that Israel is not a good ally. Nor is Israel a good friend to the American people. What ally and what friend would demand of a nation and its people to continuously support without challenge, or explanation, their nefarious plans and calculated deeds to wipe out an entire population of largely defenseless people?

The American people must demand an immediate and uncompromised end to the blind and insane U.S. support of Israel and its reprehensible and vile destruction of the Palestinian people before it is too late. The mandate and requisite road map for peace is very simple: Demand full implementation of all United Nations General Assembly and Security Council Resolutions relevant to the conflict in the Middle East and stop this inhumane and heinous carnage by the Israeli government aimed at and inflicted against the hapless and defenseless Palestinian people.

Israel's Criminal Intentions

The criminally insane Israeli government now claims it plans to expel [Palestinian leader] Yasser Arafat from Palestine, or to kill him. This announcement by the Israeli government hasn't indicated which option it will choose. But make no mistake about it, it most assuredly will happen. The Israeli government has a habit of broaching its most controversial, aka unlawful, plans in the media to head off and dilute any possible—no matter how weak and ineffectual—U.S. government opposition and to a lesser degree international opposition and to establish how ever weak of a claim that they forewarned the international community of their plans and therefore are absolved of any wrongdoing.

What right does Israel have to expel Yasser Arafat into exile? [Arafat died in 2004.] What international law and precedent allows such a move? A more odious plan of action by Israel would be the assassination—the murdering—of Arafat. [As of 2002] President Arafat has been held virtually captive in his destroyed Ramallah compound for over two years, imprisoned, under full scrutiny and observation of the IDF [Israeli Defence Force], unable to set a foot past his confines. So what precisely grants Israel impunity to do as it wishes, to whom it wishes, in complete contravention of international law, to elected leaders within the boundaries of their own land? And while under virtual house arrest, how can Arafat rightfully be held responsible for not being able to stop [the Palestinian terrorist group] Hamas, or any other act of armed resistance by any Palestinian faction?

This is another in a long list of mischievous and devious Israeli tauntings and calculated schemes of out of control spin and manipulation of on the ground facts to give credence and legitimacy to their belligerent and dastardly policies and military brutality against the Palestinians in the guise of fighting Palestinian terrorism instigated by Arafat and the Palestinian Authority.

How can the elected leader of Palestine possibly be responsible for the actions of the armed Palestinian resistance? The justification for every bit of what the Israelis has thrown at the Palestinian Intifadah [uprising] has been laid at the feet of a besieged and captive duly elected President. [George W.] Bush keeps demanding that Arafat dismantle the Palestinian terrorist infrastructure. Sharon, the yet-to-be-indicted war criminal, insists that Arafat dismantle every bit of the armed Palestinian resistance and until he does, he, as the elected Prime Minister of Israel, will continue these most sickly and despicable acts of cowardice against this small group of Arabs.

How pathetic and prophetic.

Bush, with a vast military and arsenal financed by a defense budget larger than the rest of the planet combined, cannot find one man in [the terrorist] Osama Bin Laden and after a year of continuous military action still cannot claim the dismantling of [the al Qaeda terrorist group].

Sharon Is a Criminal

Ariel 'The Butcher of Sabra and Shatilla and Qibya and Beirut and Jenin and many other places and loathsome deeds' Sharon has tried in vain to prevent the martyr operations and all to no avail—so just what is expected of Arafat? Nothing! It's all another ploy intentionally conceived and concocted to allow certain failure and another lame and predictable excuse for the Israelis to kill more innocent Arabs and perhaps this time President Arafat included.

Hamas, whose very existence and material backing comes at the hands of the Israeli government. The same which can be said of the U.S. and [former Iraqi leader] Saddam Hussein, Osama Bin Laden and myriad others and regimes before them.

Who Is the Real Terrorist?

What is the difference between state terrorism and individual terrorist acts? If we understand this difference, we'll understand also the evil nature of US policies in the Middle East and the forthcoming disasters. When [Palestinian leader] Yassir Arafat was put under siege in his offices and kept hostage by the Israeli occupation forces, he was constantly pressed into condemning terror and combating terrorism. Israel's state terrorism is defined by US officials as "self-defense," while individual suicide bombers are called terrorists.

Lev Grinberg, *AlterNet*, April 1, 2002.

Whatever plan Israel chooses would be a criminal act. But criminal acts are nothing new to Israel, its government, or many of its citizens.

And what will be the reaction of the Bush administration

to either of these options? Why should we, the American people, or for that matter the entire international community, expect any other response than what we are accustomed to by Bush in response to the crimes committed by Ariel 'The Man of Peace' Sharon and his supporters? Nothing.

If the Sharon regime proceeds with either of their plans, the response needs to bury Israel . . . and extremist Israeli support structures under a relentless fusillade and barrage of condemnation. Israel needs [to be] ostracized and isolated by sanctions from the rest of the entire international community of nations until it falls into line and stops this intentional decimation of Palestine.

Because Bush and his aides have staked a clear and visible dislike of German Chancellor Gerhard Schroeder and French President Jacques Chirac; because they would not fall into lock step with British Prime Minister Tony Blair, perhaps it is then acceptable to Bush to exercise the right to send them into exile and to forcefully do so? And to do so by sending a belligerent military force into France and Germany to extract those leaders for expulsion under heavy gunfire without conscience, or concern for the citizens of either country? There is no difference. It is just as preposterous and criminal for the Israelis in their proposition concerning Yasser Arafat.

While we are on the subject of criminality:

Violations of U.S. Laws

It is a violation of U.S. laws to provide material support for criminal and corrupt governments. Israel is in violation of near seventy UN General Assembly and Security Council Resolutions in regards to the Middle East conflict.

Under numerous scenarios, Israeli [prime minister] Ariel Sharon and numerous other Israeli officials are guilty of multitudes of violations of the Geneva Convention and other international laws, covenants and treaties. Some punishable by death.

The entirety of the House of Representatives, the U.S. Senate and the Executive Branch, including President Bush, are guilty of aiding and abetting Israel in its flagrant, intentional and willful commitment of crimes against the Palestinian people. . . .

The U.S. government has also violated numerous laws in regards to certain forms of military and financial aid provided to Israel in contravention to money laundering laws and laws regarding the structuring of all aid and the repayment/obligations of the recipient country concerning how the aid is used and the reporting requirements/accountability of all aid—military, or otherwise.

Both Israel and the United States are guilty of violations of numerous UN Resolutions concerning the treatment of Palestinian citizens and the illegal occupation of Palestinian territory.

How can anything out of the mouth of the Israeli government, or any of its politicians, or any of the supporters of the Zionist campaign, or any others who support or bless the Israeli apartheid against the Palestinian people be believed in any regard, on any matter?

For that matter, how can any U.S. politician?

Periodical Bibliography

The following articles have been selected to supplement the diverse views presented in this chapter.

Hanan Ashrawi — "Where We Went Wrong: A Palestinian's Soul Search," *Progressive*, February 2002.

Sue Boland — "Palestine: The Myth of the Empty Land," *Green Left Weekly*, April 25, 2000.

Shahul Hameed — "The Biblical Roots of the Palestinian Problem," *Islam Online*, June 12, 2003. www.islamonline.net.

Mark Harlan — "A Middle Way in the Middle East: A Third Theological Path Through the Israeli-Palestinian Thicket," *Christianity Today*, April 2003.

Tikva Honig-Parnass — "Israel's Colonial Strategies to Destroy Palestinian Nationalism," *Race and Class*, October–December 2003.

Samah Jabr — "The Palestinian Resistance: Its Legitimate Right and Moral Duty," *Washington Report on Middle East Affairs*, December 2003.

Jeff Jacoby — "Oslo's Terrible Toll," *Israel National News*, September 15, 2003.

Fiamma Nirenstein — "Israel's Last Line of Defense," *Commentary*, January 2003.

Michael B. Oren and Yossi Klein Halevi — "Jerusalem Dispatch: Fantasy," *New Republic*, December 15, 2003.

Ira Schwartz — "Jerusalem, the Holy," *Midstream*, January 2001.

Richard Webster — "Saddam, Arafat, and the Saudis Hate the Jews and Want to See Them Destroyed," *New Statesman*, December 1, 2002.

Ahmed Yasin — "Letter to the Arab Summit," www.palestine chronicle.com, April 3, 2004.

Robert Younes — "Israel's Psychological Terrorism," *Washington Report on Middle East Affairs*, March 2003.

CHAPTER 3

Is Peace Between Israel and the Palestinians Possible?

Chapter Preface

It is sometimes argued that the creation of the state of Israel imposed an artificially contrived nation on an established region. However, most of the modern nations of the Middle East were created somewhat abitrarily in the twentieth century from previously colonized lands. The seemingly arbitrary determination of these borders has led to wars between Iraq and Kuwait, Iraq and Iran, and Israel and its Arab neighbors. Ironically, many believe that the creation of one more state, Palestine, will bring peace to the region.

The conflict between Israel and the Palestinians has remained a constant since Israel's founding in 1948. Resolving the conflict is of central importance to most of the world for two reasons: the significance of the Middle East's holy sites—particularly those in Jerusalem —and the importance to the world economy of maintaining the stability of the region, which possesses much of the world's oil.

For decades, mediators from Europe, Russia, the United States, and the United Nations have proposed solutions for the Israeli-Palestinian conflict. There have been some successes, most notably the normalization of diplomatic relations between Israel and two Arab nations, Jordan and Egypt. Even these modest achievements came at a high price: the assassinations of Egyptian president Anwar Sadat and Israeli prime minister Yitzhak Rabin.

Efforts to find a solution to the conflict have become more urgent but even less successful since the September 11, 2001, terrorist attacks on America. The Israeli-Palestinian dispute is widely seen as fanning the flames of extremism. Many analysts reason that resolving the conflict could help prevent further terrorist attacks like September 11. In addition, by 2003, the United States was occupying two Muslim countries, Afghanistan and Iraq, in conducting its war on terrorism, and was eager to demonstrate to the Muslim world that it would be evenhanded in its dealings with Israel and the Palestinians. As a result, along with the United Nations, the European Union, and Russia, it proposed yet another peace plan, called the "Road Map," which, like most of the others, appears to have stalled.

Whether Israelis and Palestinians can put aside old grievances and compromise for a peaceful solution remains to be seen. Because of the hardened views of the veterans who lead each side, some believe that peace will only be possible after a new generation assumes the leadership of both Israel and the Palestinian Authority. The viewpoints in the following chapter demonstrate the complexity and difficulty of the continuing search for peace in the Middle East.

"A State of Palestine alongside the State of Israel, with both peoples living in peace, would fulfill the basic aspirations of both peoples."

Peace Between Israel and the Palestinians Is Possible

Ziad Asali

In the following viewpoint, Ziad Asali argues that peace between Israel and the Palestinians is possible if both sides compromise. He offers a plan for such a compromise that would create a Palestinian state alongside Israel based on the borders in existence in 1967 and a divided Jerusalem. He cautions that peace can only be achieved if the United States acts as a forceful broker and if the North Atlantic Treaty Organization or other forces provide security guarantees. Ziad Asali is president of the American-Arab Anti-Discrimination Committee.

As you read, consider the following questions:

1. According to the author, what historically was the dream of the Jewish people?
2. According to the author, what is the goal of the Palestinian people?
3. What does the author mean by "the ideology of collective victimization"?

Ziad Asali, "In Pursuit of Peace (Beyond the Road Map)," *Tikkun*, July/August 2003. Copyright © 2003 by the Institute for Labor and Mental Health. Reprinted by permission of *Tikkun*: A Bimonthly Jewish Critique of Politics, Culture & Society.

The march of events that we call history has been unkind to both Jews and Palestinians [in the twentieth] century. Europe, the seat of world culture and western civilization, was seized with convulsive fits of hatred and barbarism that culminated in the Holocaust and made the defeat of Nazism the highest moral order of the time. The Palestinians, caught in the ensuing whirlwind, were eviscerated, displaced, denigrated, and driven to desperation. Israel was established on 78 percent of the land of Palestine in 1948, and occupied the rest in 1967.

Much of what happened over the past several decades in these geographic confines that accommodate two peoples and three religions was a clash of narratives, a consequence of each side's belief in its exclusive possession of pain and suffering, its monopoly of victimization. The pain of the others was not only unfelt but rather has become a source of lust recompense for the pain they inflict. Revenge, of biblical proportion, primitive and all consuming, has engulfed an ever-increasing circle of adherents within a maddening spiral of violence, mayhem and death. Individual responsibility has dissolved into a group ethos of hostility, undifferentiated and dominant. Individuals and tiny groups who have searched for a compromise out of this sad mess have been marginalized and rendered ineffectual.

Real Estate

The Palestinian/Israeli conflict can be viewed simply, and simplistically, as a real estate deal whose contract is being negotiated with blood. The problem with this construct is that the title deed for both people becomes religious texts and dogma, thus introducing all the metaphysical forces, perceived, imagined, or felt, by Jews, Christians, and Muslims of all times. Such a view takes the conflict outside the realm of time, both the past and the future, and ordains it to an eternal struggle. No sane person would see that as a legacy worthy of this generation to bequeath to our progeny.

Most of us, mortals with no claim to direct communication with the divinity, more encumbered with respect for law, justice, and peace than with visions of heaven on earth, cannot watch with indifference the workings of the extremists and zealots. It is indeed our obligation to present the world with a better vision for the future than that of the "clashists" (as in Fascists), whose visions of Apocalypse and Armageddon compel them to achieve the glorious end of fire and destruction in Palestine.

The problem with history is that it has been around for a long time. It provides endless examples, lessons, and justifications for each action or plan imagined by humans. Add religion to that story and you get the history of the Holy Land. Add nationality as yet another layer of complexity and you get the history of the Palestine/Israel conflict. Add the current events created by live human beings fighting with no self-imposed limits for what they perceive to be their existence, security, and dignity, and you will have a sense why it is beyond the realm of the possible to expect the victimized people of Israel and Palestine to resolve this conflict if left to their own devices. Like abused children, these two peoples in their collectivity and by themselves are hurt beyond reason and compromise. There seems to be no end to their ability to test each other's limits of suffering and pain. A grown-up needs to intervene and put an end to this conflict.

The Jewish people have held on to their dream of going back to Palestine for ages as they endured the calumny of anti-Semitism and a Diaspora of the soul. They wanted nothing other than to live by themselves and take care of themselves. They achieved that by establishing Israel in 1948, but their achievement continues to be contested. The Palestinian people, through no fault of their own, lost control of their ancestral land, homes, farms, villages, and cities as well as their identity as a people in 1948. They happened to live in a place desired and claimed by Jews fleeing an anti-Semitic Europe and welcome nowhere else. Enduring with uncommon valor and tenacity, they have held on to the dream of having their own country, living by themselves and taking care of themselves.

A Historic Compromise

There is room in this world, and in historic Palestine, to accommodate these two dreams in a historic compromise. A State of Palestine alongside the State of Israel, with both peoples living in peace, would fulfill the basic aspirations of both peoples. The basic fear of Palestinians is to end up without a state—a genuine, viable, independent, constitutional state of their own choosing, and not be cheated out of it by guile or uneven power. The basic fear of Israel is to be rejected and destroyed in the future by a hostile Arab and Islamic world after it makes concessions that might make it less secure and more vulnerable. Noises made by extremists and clashists on all sides do nothing to allay those fears. The fact that these noises do nothing to change the status quo, or to advance any cause, is less often noted or mentioned.

The two-state solution addresses the legitimate, fundamental fears of both peoples and cannot be abandoned because violent men, on either side, are allowed to exercise their veto power by unleashing their deadly wares.

The outlines of the historic compromise are:

1. Establishing a state of Palestine alongside Israel based on the borders of 1967 with mutually agreed border modifications.
2. A shared Jerusalem with Arab East Jerusalem serving as capital of Palestine and West Jerusalem serving as capital of Israel.
3. A fair solution of the refugee problem based on international law and relevant United Nations resolutions to be negotiated between the parties.
4. The end of occupation and evacuation of settlements.
5. Signed peace treaties between Israel and all Arab states based on the Saudi proposal adopted by the Arab League.
6. A . . . plan to rebuild Palestine and the new Middle East.

International Support

The broad contours of this compromise have been supported by the United States, the United Nations, the European Union, the Arab League and seem to get the support of the Israeli and Palestinian people as evidenced by surveys. Perhaps the most contentious issue is the right of return, which is a right that property owners have that cannot be abrogated without their consent. This right is not the same as the actual physical return of the refugees. Serious people will

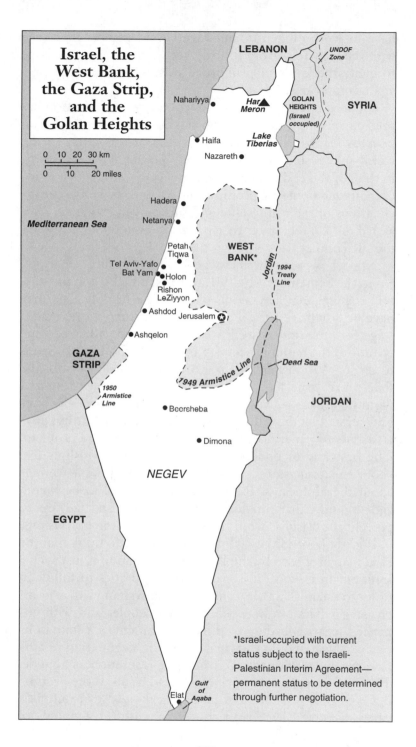

Israel, the
West Bank,
the Gaza Strip,
and the
Golan Heights

0   10 20 30 km
0   10   20 miles

LEBANON

UNDOF
Zone

Nahariyya

Har
Meron

GOLAN
HEIGHTS
(Israeli
occupied)

SYRIA

Haifa

Lake
Tiberias

Nazareth

Mediterranean Sea

Hadera

Netanya

Petah
Tiqwa

WEST
BANK*

Jordan

1994
Treaty
Line

Tel Aviv-Yafo
Bat Yam

Holon

Rishon
LeZiyyon

Ashdod

Jerusalem

Ashqelon

GAZA
STRIP

1950
Armistice
Line

1949 Armistice Line

Dead Sea

JORDAN

Beersheba

Dimona

NEGEV

EGYPT

*Israeli-occupied with current
status subject to the Israeli-
Palestinian Interim Agreement—
permanent status to be determined
through further negotiation.

Elat

Gulf
of
Aqaba

111

have to work diligently and together to resolve this issue with the view to solving it justly, rather than using the issue to incite the kinds of primordial existential fears that preclude compromise.

Up until now, the ideology of collective victimization has precluded compromise and allowed the extremists to play on people's fears. The United States, the only country in the world able to step into this conflict, has not acted decisively, in spite of the crying need to do so. Global strategic considerations and domestic political calculations, as well as the inclinations of the ruling elite and successive presidents, have all led the United States to avoid a serious attempt at resolving the conflict.

Now, however, the new geopolitical reality emerging from [the September 11, 2001, terrorist attacks] and the seismic changes that are taking place in the Middle East may have at last placed the Palestine/Israel issue at the center stage for attention as well as action. Indeed, it has become critical to the national security interest of the United States to do so. Within much of the Arab and Muslim world, the Palestinian issue has represented people's sense of injured dignity, weakness, vulnerability, and impotence—feelings exaggerated by the failure of corrupt Arab and Muslim governments to pay little more than lip service to the problem. The best way to understand how Arabs and Muslims feel about this issue is to compare it with the Jewish feelings about the Holocaust. Rational solutions need to be found, and urgently, that provide a sense of hope and fairness to prevent the clashists from realizing their apocalyptic visions.

It is not beyond the realm of the possible to think that the road map proposed by the Bush administration is just such a solution. In essence, it is a map for the parties to follow in order to establish a Palestinian political system, with ever increasing separation between the two peoples and with enhanced security leading to the establishment of a state in its second stage, and, in the final stage, the negotiation of a final agreement with the Arab League resolution as a guide. The road map could, in principle, lead us all to the promising land of peace. It could just as easily lead us to unmitigated disaster. I have read with great care the opinions of scholars, seasoned politicians, and hard-nosed ideologues who paint with painful detail all the ways in which this road map can be derailed and abused and lead to a dead end. This all may turn out to be true, but it is also true that the road map is the only game in town.

Outside Intervention

It is my contention that the parties themselves are inherently unable to resolve this conflict on their own, not just because of individual or mass psychology, but also because of the flagrant imbalance of power between the two parties. The United States has to be more than the "honest broker" of bygone days. It has to be honest, and it has to be a broker. The fundamental issue of security cannot be left to locals to implement. Outside forces, strictly controlled by the United States, perhaps under NATO [North Atlantic Treaty Organization] or other friendly forces, can play a constructive role in resolving this thorny issue. Without a sense of full security, Israel cannot be made to move. Without a sense of full independence, the Palestinians will not yield. With a force of international peacekeepers, it is entirely possible to accommodate both.

A non-belligerent, viable, Palestinian State, with the substance and trappings of independence, would be the single most stabilizing source of security in the Middle East. Peace, genuine peace in the hearts and minds of people, like the one that has existed between the French and Germans in Europe after the Second World War, will not be far behind the establishment of such a state. To achieve this outcome, however, we must plan for that peace and prevent others from derailing it. The enterprising Israeli people will need to work to erase the memory of occupation from the Palestinians. The resilient Palestinians will have to re-earn the trust of the Israelis who suffered from suicide bombing. Time, and good will on the part of many, will make such things possible.

Peace in Our Time?

Is it possible to have peace in our time? Other than wishing for a positive answer, we cannot provide a meaningful response. Perhaps the more relevant question is: What can we, as citizens, do to make it happen?

Those of us who are roughly in agreement on the contours of the solution need to work together, speaking up, organizing, and pushing this agenda of peace to all levels within our reach. Palestinian and Jewish Americans have a particular responsibility to tell the world that the majority of the people within our communities are for peace. We refuse to be divided simply along religious and tribal affiliations that define our stand on issues. The resolution of this conflict is not a zero sum game. The future of all Palestinian and Israeli children will be brighter if we make an honorable peace.

We also should break the taboo of not speaking to each other, in the open and forthrightly. We should not shrink from telling each other what we think. What the Palestinians think is that occupation is the source of all troubles and all other issues will dissipate as it comes to an end. We understand that for the Israelis, security is the main issue that dwarfs all others. It is our role as American citizens to work together to help the parties untie this Gordian knot. It is our obligation to see to it that our country does the right thing, for our sake and for the sake of the Israelis; for the sake of the Palestinians, the Arabs, and the Muslims; and, indeed, for the sake of the world at large.

We should see to it that our opinions are heard at the White House, the State Department, the hallways of the Congress, on the evening news, in the editorial pages, in colleges and in barbershops across the nation. Man-made conflicts are to be resolved by men and women. We cannot accept a religious and tribal feud that defines us beyond the realm of time. We will say to each other and to all who want to listen that we will extend a hand, and will take a chance on each other, and will work together for peace. Of course, individuals will let each other down—that has happened in the past and it forever will. But no progress, no peace, and no bright future will be there for our children if we fail to act now.

Let politicians in Palestine and Israel work to sort out their strategies, but let us here and now work on our own administration and our Congress to see to it that the vision of peace articulated by the president is translated into reality. In particular, now that the president has expressed his personal commitment, as well as his administration's, to making the road map work, we must labor to make sure his commitment does not waver. Let us not allow those who are steeped in mistrust and fear on either side make the world lose once again another opportunity for peace.

A thousand flowers are blooming across our country with voices for peace, interfaith groups, Arab-Jewish dialogue, Muslim Christian groups, and Palestinians talking to Jews about peace. Let us light those candles with courage and not in fear. A future defined by our vision and our energy is well worthy of our toil.

*"[Jewish] concessions confronted
[Palestinian Authority chairman Yasser]
Arafat with the one outcome he did not
want: peace with Israel."*

Peace Between Israel and the Palestinians Is Not Possible

David Horowitz

In the following viewpoint, David Horowitz argues that the Palestinian-Israeli conflict is not about the Palestinians' desire for a state. Rather, it is about the desire of the Arabs to destroy the state of Israel. He claims that the Arab nations have intentionally kept Palestinian refugees in deplorable camps to incite hatred of Israel. According to the author, peace between Israel and the Palestinians is impossible because the Arabs will settle for nothing less than the annihilation of Israel. David Horowitz is the author of several books, including *Left Illusions*.

As you read, consider the following questions:
1. What country does the author believe should be the homeland of the Palestinians?
2. According to its original charter, what was the goal of the Palestine Liberation Organization, as reported by the author?
3. According to the author, what actions did each side take after signing the Oslo Accords?

David Horowitz, "Horowitz's Notepad: Why Israel Is the Victim and the Arabs Are the Indefensible Aggressors in the Middle East," www.frontpagemag.com, January 11, 2000. Copyright © 2000 by the Center for the Study of Popular Culture. Reproduced by permission.

The Middle East conflict is not about Israel's occupation of the territories; it is about the refusal of the Arabs to make peace with Israel, which is an inevitable by-product of their desire to destroy it.

The Palestinians and their supporters . . . claim that the Middle East conflict is about the Palestinians' yearning for a state and the refusal of Israel to accept their aspiration. This claim is also false. The Palestine Liberation Organization was created in 1964, sixteen years after the establishment of Israel and the first anti-Israel war. The PLO was created at a time the West Bank was not under Israeli control but was part of Jordan. The PLO, however, was not created so that the Palestinians could achieve self-determination in Jordan, which at the time comprised 90 percent of the original Palestine Mandate. The PLO's express purpose, in the words of its own leaders, was to "push the Jews into the sea."

The official charter of the new Palestine Liberation Organization referred to the "Zionist invasion," declared that Israel's Jews were "not an independent nationality," described Zionism as "racist" and "fascist," called for "the liquidation of the Zionist presence," and specified, "armed struggle is the only way to liberate Palestine." In short, "liberation" required the destruction of the Jewish state. The PLO was not even created by Palestinians but by the Arab League—the corrupt dictators who ruled the Middle East and who had attempted to destroy Israel by military force in 1948, in 1967 and again in 1973.

For thirty years, the PLO charter remained unchanged in its call for Israel's destruction. Then in the mid-1990s, under enormous international pressure following the 1993 Oslo accords, PLO leader Yasser Arafat removed the clause while assuring his followers that its removal was a necessary compromise that did not alter the movement's goals. He did this explicitly and also by citing a historical precedent in which the Prophet Muhammad insincerely agreed to a peace with his enemies in order to gain time to mass the forces with which he intended to destroy them.

The Middle East struggle is not about right against right. It is about a fifty-year effort by the Arabs to destroy the Jewish state, and the refusal of the Arab states in general and the

Palestinian Arabs in particular to accept Israel's existence. If the Arabs were willing to do this, there would be no occupied territories and there would be a Palestinian state.

Even during the "Oslo" peace process—when the Palestine Liberation Organization pretended to recognize the existence of Israel and the Jews therefore allowed the creation of a "Palestine Authority"—it was clear that the PLO's goal was Israel's destruction, and not just because its leader invoked the Prophet Muhammad's own deception. The Palestinians' determination to destroy Israel is abundantly clear in their newly created demand of a "right of return" to Israel for "5 million" Arabs. The figure of 5 million refugees who must be returned to Israel is more than *ten* times the number of Arabs who actually left the Jewish slivers of the British Mandate in 1948.

Right of Return

In addition to its absurdity, this new demand has several aspects that reveal the Palestinians' genocidal agenda for the Jews. The first is that the "right of return" is itself a calculated mockery of the primary reason for Israel's existence—the fact that no country would provide a refuge for Jews fleeing Hitler's extermination program during World War II. It is only because the world turned its back on the Jews when their survival was at stake that the state of Israel grants a "right of return" to every Jew who asks for it.

But there is no genocidal threat to Arabs, no lack of international support militarily and economically, and no Palestinian "diaspora" (although the Palestinians have cynically appropriated the very term to describe their self-inflicted quandary). The fact that many Arabs, including the Palestinian spiritual leader—the Grand Mufti of Jerusalem—supported Hitler's "Final Solution" only serves to compound the insult. It is even further compounded by the fact that more than 90 percent of the Palestinians now in the West Bank and Gaza have never lived a day of their lives in territorial Israel. The claim of a "right of return" is thus little more than a brazen expression of contempt for the Jews, and for their historic suffering.

More importantly it is an expression of contempt for the

very idea of a Jewish state. The incorporation of five million Arabs into Israel would render the Jews a permanent minority in their own country, and would thus spell the end of Israel. The Arabs fully understand this, and that is why they have made it a fundamental demand. It is just one more instance of the general bad faith the Arab side has manifested through every chapter of these tragic events.

Possibly the most glaring expression of the Arabs' bad faith is their deplorable treatment of the Palestinian refugees and refusal for half a century to relocate them, or to alleviate their condition, even during the years they were under Jordanian rule. While Israel was making the desert bloom and relocating 600,000 Jewish refugees from Arab states, and building a thriving industrial democracy in its allotted sliver, the Arabs were busy making sure that *their* refugees remained in squalid refugee camps in the West Bank and Gaza, where they were powerless, right-less, and economically destitute.

Today, fifty years after the first Arab war against Israel, there are 59 such refugee camps and 3.7 million "refugees" registered with the UN [United Nations]. Despite economic aid from the UN and Israel itself, despite the oil wealth of the Arab kingdoms, the Arab leaders have refused to undertake the efforts that would liberate the refugees from their miserable camps, or to make the economic investment that would alleviate their condition. There are now 22 Arab states providing homes for the same ethnic population, speaking a common Arabic language. But the only one that will allow Palestinian Arabs to become citizens is Jordan. And the only state the Palestinians covet is Israel.

The Policy of Resentment and Hate

The refusal to address the condition of the Palestinian refugee population is—and has always been—a calculated Arab policy, intended to keep the Palestinians in a state of desperation in order to incite their hatred of Israel for the wars to come. Not to leave anything to chance, the mosques and schools of the Arabs generally—and the Palestinians in particular—preach and teach Jew hatred every day. Elementary school children in Palestinian Arab schools are even taught to chant "Death to the heathen Jews" in their class-rooms as they are learning to read. It should not be over-looked, that these twin policies of deprivation (of the Pales-tinian Arabs) and hatred (of the Jews) are carried out without any protest from any sector of Palestinian or Arab society. That in itself speaks volumes about the nature of the Middle East conflict.

Ramirez. Copyright © 2002 by the *Los Angeles Times*. Reproduced by per-mission.

All wars—especially wars that have gone on for fifty years—produce victims with just grievances on both sides. And that is true in this one. There are plenty of individual Palestinian vic-tims, as there are Jewish victims, familiar from the nightly news. But the collective Palestinian grievance is without jus-tice. It is a self-inflicted wound, the product of the Arabs' xenophobia, bigotry, exploitation of their own people, and ap-parent inability to be generous towards those who are not Arabs. While Israel is an open, democratic, multi-ethnic, mul-ticultural society that includes a large enfranchised Arab mi-nority, the Palestine Authority is an intolerant, undemocratic, monolithic police state with one dictatorial leader, whose ru-inous career has run now for [approximately] 37 years.

As the repellent attitudes, criminal methods and dishonest goals of the Palestine liberation movement should make clear to any reasonable observer, its present cause is based on Jew hatred, and on resentment of the modern, democratic West, and little else. Since there was no Palestinian nation before the creation of Israel, and since Palestinians regarded themselves simply as Arabs and their land as part of Syria, it is not surprising that many of the chief creators of the Palestine Liberation Organization did not even live in the Palestine Mandate before the creation of Israel, let alone in the sliver of mostly desert that was allotted to the Jews. Edward Said, the leading intellectual mouthpiece for the Palestinian cause grew up in a family that chose to make its home in Egypt and the United States. [Former Palestinian Authority leader] Yasser Arafat was born in Egypt.

While the same Arab states that claim to be outraged by the Jews' treatment of Palestinians treat their own Arab populations far worse than Arabs are treated in Israel, they are also silent about the disenfranchised Palestinian majority that lives in Jordan. In 1970, Jordan's King Hussein massacred thousands of PLO militants. But the PLO does not call for the overthrow of Hashemite rule in Jordan and does not hate the Hashemite monarchy. Only Jews are hated.

It is a hatred, moreover, that is increasingly lethal. Today, 70 percent of the Arabs in the West Bank and Gaza approve the suicide bombing of women and children if the targets are Jews. There is no Arab "Peace Now" movement, not even a small one, whereas in Israel the movement demanding concessions to Arabs in the name of peace is a formidable political force. There is no Arab spokesman who will speak for the rights and sufferings of Jews, but there are hundreds of thousands of Jews in Israel—and all over the world—who will speak for "justice" for the Palestinians. How can the Jews expect fair treatment from a people that collectively does not even recognize their humanity?

A Phony Peace

The Oslo peace process begun in 1993 was based on the pledge of both parties to renounce violence as a means of settling their dispute. But the Palestinians never renounced violence and in the year 2000, they officially launched a new

Intifada [holy war] against Israel, effectively terminating the peace process.

In fact, *during* the peace process—between 1993 and 1999—there were over 4,000 terrorist incidents committed by Palestinians against Israelis, and more than 1,000 Israelis killed as a result of Palestinian attacks—more than had been killed in the previous 25 years. By contrast, during the same period 1993–1999 Israelis were so desperate for peace that they reciprocated these acts of murder by giving the Palestinians in the West Bank and Gaza a self-governing authority, a 40,000 man armed "police force," and 95 percent of the territory their negotiators demanded. This Israeli generosity was rewarded by a rejection of peace, suicide bombings of crowded discos and shopping malls, an outpouring of ethnic hatred and a renewed declaration of war.

In fact, the Palestinians broke the Oslo Accords precisely *because* of Israeli generosity, *because* the government of Ehud Barak offered to meet 95 percent of their demands, including turning over parts of Jerusalem to their control—a possibility once considered unthinkable. These concessions confronted Arafat with the one outcome he did not want: peace with Israel. Peace without the destruction of the "Jewish Entity."

Arafat rejected these Israeli concessions, accompanying his rejection with a new explosion of anti-Jewish violence. He named this violence—deviously—"The Al-Aksa Intifada," after the mosque on the Temple Mount. His new *jihad* was given the name of a Muslim shrine to create the illusion that the Intifada was provoked not by his unilateral destruction of the Oslo peace process, but by [Israel leader] Ariel Sharon's visit to the site. Months after the Intifada began, the Palestine Authority itself admitted this was just another Arafat lie.

In fact, the Intifada had been planned months before Sharon's visit as a follow-up to the rejection of the Oslo Accords. In the words of Imad Faluji, the Palestine Authority's communications minister, "[The uprising] had been planned since Chairman Arafat's return from Camp David, when he turned the tables on the former U.S. president [Bill Clinton] and rejected the American conditions." The same conclusion was reached by the Mitchell Commission headed by former

U.S. Senator George Mitchell to investigate the events: "The Sharon visit did not cause the Al-Aksa Intifada."

Moral Distinctions

In assessing the Middle East impasse it is important to pay attention to the moral distinction revealed in the actions of the two combatants. When a deranged Jew goes into an Arab mosque and kills the worshippers (which happened *once*) he is acting alone and is universally condemned by the Israeli government and the Jews in Israel and everywhere, and he is punished to the full extent of Israeli law. But when a young Arab enters a disco filled with teenagers or a shopping mall or bus crowded with women and children and blows himself and innocent bystanders up (which happens frequently), he is someone who has been trained and sent by a component of the PLO or the Palestine Authority; he is officially praised as a hero by Yasser Arafat; his mother is given money by the Palestine Authority; and his Arab neighbors come to pay honor to the household for having produced a "martyr for Allah." The Palestinian liberation movement is the first such movement to elevate the killing of children—both the enemy's and its own—into a religious calling and a strategy of the cause.

It is not only the methods of the Palestine liberation movement that are morally repellent. The Palestinian cause is itself corrupt. The "Palestinian problem" is a problem created by the Arabs, and can only be solved by them. In Jordan, Palestinians already have a state in which they are a majority but which denies them self-determination. Why is Jordan not the object of the Palestinian "liberation" struggle? The only possible answer is *because it is not ruled by Jews.*

There is a famous "green line" marking the boundary between Israel and its Arab neighbors. That green line is also the bottom line for what is the real problem in the Middle East. It is green because plants are growing in the desert on the Israeli side but not on the Arab side. The Jews got a sliver of land without oil, and created abundant wealth and life in all its rich and diverse forms. The Arabs got nine times the acreage but all they have done with it is to sit on its aridity and nurture the poverty, resentments and hatreds of its inhabitants. Out of these dark elements they have created and perfected the most vile anti-human terrorism the world has ever seen: Suicide bombing of civilians. In fact, the Palestinians are a community of suicide bombers: they want the destruction of Israel more than they want a better life.

If a nation state is all the Palestinians desire, Jordan would be the solution. (So would settling for 95 percent of one's demands.) But the Palestinians also want to destroy Israel. This is morally hateful. It is the Nazi virus revived. Nonetheless, the Palestinian cause is generally supported by the international community, with the singular exception of the United States (and to a lesser degree Great Britain). It is precisely because the Palestinians want to destroy a state that Jews have created—and because they are killing Jews—that they enjoy international credibility and otherwise inexplicable support.

It is this international resistance to the cause of Jewish survival, the persistence of global Jew-hatred that, in the end, refutes the Zionist hope of a solution to the "Jewish problem." The creation of Israel is an awe-inspiring human success story. But the permanent war to destroy it undermines the original Zionist idea.

VIEWPOINT

"The two-state vision and the roadmap for peace . . . command nearly universal support as the best means of achieving a permanent peace."

A Two-State Solution Will Bring Peace

George W. Bush

George W. Bush was inaugurated as the forty-third president of the United States in 2001. He was the first U.S. president to officially support the creation of a Palestinian state. In the following viewpoint he argues that the creation of a peaceful Palestinian state alongside Israel will bring an end to years of conflict. He states that this two-state solution is the best path to peace, and maintains that ending the conflict will benefit the entire region.

As you read, consider the following questions:
1. According to the author, what are the Palestinians' obligations?
2. According to Bush, what are Israel's obligations?
3. How does the author think Israel's security fence should be used?

George W. Bush, statement, Washington, DC, April 14, 2004.

125

I remain hopeful and determined to find a way forward toward a resolution of the Israeli-Palestinian dispute.

The Israeli Plan

I welcome the disengagement plan prepared by the Government of Israel, under which Israel would withdraw certain military installations and all settlements from Gaza, and withdraw certain military installations and settlements in the West Bank. These steps will mark real progress toward realizing the vision I set forth in June 2002 of two states living side by side in peace and security, and make a real contribution toward peace.

I am hopeful that steps pursuant to this plan, consistent with this vision, will remind all states and parties of their own obligations under the roadmap [the name for this two-state plan].

The Path to Peace

I believe certain principles, which are very widely accepted in the international community, show us the path forward: The right of self defense and the need to fight terrorism are equally matters of international agreement. The two-state vision and the roadmap for peace designed to implement it, command nearly universal support as the best means of achieving a permanent peace and an end to the Israeli occupation that began in 1967. United Nations Security Council resolutions have repeatedly spoken of the desirability of establishing two independent states, Israel and Palestine, living side by side within secure and recognized borders.

Having these principles in mind, the United States is able to make the following comments.

Peace Plans

The United States remains committed to the vision of two states living side by side in peace and security, and its implementation as described in the roadmap. The United States will do its utmost to prevent any attempt by anyone to impose any other plan.

There will be no security for Israelis or Palestinians until they and all states, in the region and beyond, join together to fight terrorism and dismantle terrorist organizations. The United States reiterates its steadfast commitment to Israel's security, including secure, defensible borders, and to preserve and strengthen Israel's capability to deter and defend itself, by itself, against any threat or possible combination of threats. The United States will join with others in the international community to strengthen the capacity and will of Palestinian security forces to fight terrorism and dismantle terrorist capabilities and infrastructure.

Terrorism

Israel will retain its right to defend itself against terrorism, including to take actions against terrorist organizations. The United States will lead efforts, working together with Jordan, Egypt, and others in the international community, to build the capacity and will of Palestinian institutions to fight terrorism, dismantle terrorist organizations, and prevent the areas from which Israel has withdrawn from posing a threat that would have to be addressed by any other means. The United States understands that after Israel withdraws from Gaza and/or parts of the West Bank, and pending agreements on other arrangements, existing arrangements regarding control of airspace, territorial waters, and land passages of the West Bank and Gaza will continue.

The Two-State Solution

The United States remains committed to the two-state solution for peace in the Middle East as set forth in June 2002, and to the roadmap as the best path to realize that vision.

The goal of two independent states has repeatedly been recognized in international resolutions and agreements, and it remains a key to resolving this conflict. The United States is strongly committed to Israel's security and well-being as a Jewish state. It seems clear that an agreed, just, fair and realistic framework for a solution to the Palestinian refugee issue as part of any final status agreement will need to be found through the establishment of a Palestinian state, and the settling of Palestinian refugees there, rather than in Israel.

As part of a final peace settlement, Israel must have secure and recognized borders, which should emerge from negoti-

Palestinian Self-Government

I take this opportunity to appeal to the Palestinians and repeat, as I said at Aqaba: it is not in our interest to govern you. We would like you to govern yourselves in your own country; a democratic Palestinian state. . . .

The Road Map is the only political plan accepted by Israel, the Palestinians, the Americans and a majority of the international community. We are willing to proceed toward its implementation: two states—Israel and a Palestinian state—living side by side in tranquility, security and peace.

Ariel Sharon, December 18, 2003, www.aipac.org.

ations between the parties in accordance with UNSC [UN Security Council] Resolutions 242 and 338. In light of new realities on the ground, including already existing major Israeli populations centers, it is unrealistic to expect that the outcome of final status negotiations will be a full and complete return to the armistice lines of 1949, and all previous efforts to negotiate a two-state solution have reached the same conclusion. It is realistic to expect that any final status agreement will only be achieved on the basis of mutually agreed changes that reflect these realities.

Palestinian Statehood

The United States supports the establishment of a Palestinian state that is viable, contiguous, sovereign, and independent, so that the Palestinian people can build their own future in accordance with the vision I set forth in June 2002 and with the path set forth in the roadmap. The United States will join with others in the international community to foster the development of democratic political institutions and new leadership committed to those institutions, the reconstruction of civic institutions, the growth of a free and prosperous economy, and the building of capable security institutions dedicated to maintaining law and order and dismantling terrorist organizations.

Palestinian Obligations

Under the roadmap, Palestinians must undertake an immediate cessation of armed activity and all acts of violence against

Israelis anywhere, and all official Palestinian institutions must end incitement against Israel. The Palestinian leadership must act decisively against terror, including sustained, targeted, and effective operations to stop terrorism and dismantle terrorist capabilities and infrastructure. Palestinians must undertake a comprehensive and fundamental political reform that includes a strong parliamentary democracy and an empowered prime minister.

Israeli Obligations

The Government of Israel is committed to take additional steps on the West Bank, including progress toward a freeze on settlement activity, removing unauthorized outposts, and improving the humanitarian situation by easing restrictions on the movement of Palestinians not engaged in terrorist activities.

As the Government of Israel has stated, the barrier being erected by Israel should be a security rather than political barrier, should be temporary rather than permanent, and therefore not prejudice any final status issues including final borders, and its route should take into account, consistent with security needs, its impact on Palestinians not engaged in terrorist activities.

Regional Cooperation

A peace settlement negotiated between Israelis and Palestinians would be a great boon not only to those peoples but to the peoples of the entire region. Accordingly, all states in the region have special responsibilities: to support the building of the institutions of a Palestinian state; to fight terrorism, and cut off all forms of assistance to individuals and groups engaged in terrorism; and to begin now to move toward more normal relations with the State of Israel. These actions would be true contributions to building peace in the region.

"Even if Arafat & Co. scrupulously adhered to The Road Map's conditions, a Palestinian state would still be the grave of Israel."

A Two-State Solution Will Not Create Peace

Don Feder

Don Feder is a syndicated columnist who frequently writes about the Middle East. In the following viewpoint, he criticizes the most recent American peace plan for the Middle East, the "Road Map," for requiring what he calls "suicidal concessions" from Israel. Feder questions the need for a new Palestinian state, when one already exists—Jordan. He argues that the new Palestinian state would become a staging ground for Arab conquest of "greater Palestine," resulting in the death of the state of Israel.

As you read, consider the following questions:
1. According to Feder, what was Saddam Hussein's connection to the Palestinians?
2. What does the author mean by PLO chairman Arafat's "phased plan"?
3. According to the author, what role does religion play in the Israeli-Palestinian conflict?

In his Feb. 26 [2003] speech to the American Enterprise Institute, President George W. Bush predicted, "Success in Iraq [to depose Iraqi leader Saddam Hussein] could also begin a new stage in Middle Eastern peace and set in motion progress toward a truly democratic Palestinian state." He then gave his "personal commitment" to The Road Map, a plan concocted by Russia, the European Union and United Nations for an imposed settlement of the Israeli-Palestinian conflict.

This plan calls for a number of interim steps toward the imposition of a Palestinian state "containing the maximum contiguous territory." Israel is to have no control over the borders and airspace of "Palestine," thus no control over the importation of military hardware from throughout the Arab world.

This envisioned 23rd Arab state is to be created in two stages. Following elections, there will be a state with temporary borders and international recognition by the end of 2003. Permanent borders are to be established after the resolution of such thorny issues as the so-called right of return (the Palestinian demand to flood the rest of Israel with hundreds of thousands of refugees and their descendants), the status of Jerusalem and the fate of 250,000 Jews living in Arafatistan [coined after former Palestinian Authority leader Yasir Arafat].

In his June 24, 2002 speech, the president assured us that a Palestinian state would only come after the removal of Arafat, the election of a new leadership "not compromised by terrorism," the cessation of all terrorist acts and an end to incitement by the Palestinian Authority. Other than some window dressing—Arafat appointing his colleague Mahmoud Abbas (a Holocaust denier who supports the murder of Jews on the West Bank) prime minister of the PA—none of those conditions have been met.

Still, the administration has announced that as soon as the [Iraq] war is over, it will begin to push for implementation of The Road Map. Based on past experience, expect token efforts to be accepted as Palestinian compliance, while suicidal concessions are demanded of Israel.

No matter. Even if Arafat & Co. scrupulously adhered to The Road Map's conditions, a Palestinian state would still be the grave of Israel.

To understand why, consider what's been going on in the Palestinian Authority since the Iraq war started. Demonstrators have crowded the streets chanting, "Death to America. Death to Bush." An official of Arafat's PLO told Al-Jazeera TV, "Iraq's battle is Palestine's battle."

Fiery sermons are regularly broadcast on Palestinian television, including one by Sheikh Ibrahim Mudayris expressing the hope that "Americans will drown in their own blood." The PA renamed a city square in Jenin to honor the suicide bomber who murdered four American soldiers on March 27th [2003].

Hamas (a member of Arafat's PLO) enlisted terrorists to fight U.S. forces in Iraq. And Arafat sent Saddam his "warmest greetings" and "deepest prayers to Allah, may He . . . strengthen our brotherly ties, cooperation and solidarity." In the past, those brotherly ties have included Arafat's active support for Iraq in the Persian Gulf War and Saddam paying $25,000 bounties to the families of Palestinian suicide bombers.

Palestinian Terrorism

This is the face of a future Palestinian state—not the diplomatic delusions of a peaceful and democratic Palestine living in harmony with Israel—but fundamentalism, irredentism and terrorism.

Since [the Oslo peace accords], the Palestinians have given every indication that they will follow in the footsteps of every other Middle East tyranny. The Palestinian Authority inculcates virulent anti-Semitism in its media, school curriculum and religious broadcasts. Since September 2000, Palestinians have murdered 761 Jews and wounded more than 5,000—almost 80 percent civilians. A March 8, 2003 poll showed 70% of Palestinians support these atrocities.

Why a Palestinian State?

Yes, but the Palestinians must have a nation of their own, the international community insists. Why? The "Palestinian people" is an invention of Arab propagandists. PLO [Palestine Liberation Organization] executive committee member Zahir Muhsein admitted this in a 1977 interview with a

Dutch magazine. ("Only for political reasons do we speak today about the existence of a Palestinian people, since Arab national interests demand that we posit the existence of a distinct Palestinian people to oppose Zionism.")

Arab inhabitants of Israel speak the same language, practice the same religion and observe the same customs as Arab Moslems throughout the region. They would be completely at home anywhere in the Middle East.

In the 1920s, the British lopped off 77 percent of Mandate Palestine and presented it to the Hashmite dynasty. It became Trans Jordan, later the Kingdom of Jordan. If there is a Palestinian Arab homeland, it is located on the East Bank of the Jordan.

There has never been an independent Arab state on any of the land designated the West Bank—or on the rest of Israel, for that matter. The territory targeted for a Palestinian state was illegally occupied by Jordan for 19 years and liberated by Israel in 1967. It is Biblical Israel (Abraham is buried in Hebron, not Tel Aviv)—the land promised by God to Abraham's descendants in perpetuity. Moslems currently control 99.9 percent of the land in the Middle East. Including the West Bank and Gaza, the Jews have a nation half the size of California's San Bernardino County.

Land for Peace Will Not Work

A Palestinian state living in peace and harmony with Israel? But, of course—just the way Nazi Germany peacefully coexisted with the rump Czech state, after Hitler acquired the Sudatenland. Land for peace has a distinguished lineage.

Speaking to Arab audiences, Arafat frequently refers to the "phased plan," a strategy adopted by the PLO in 1974. In an interview with Jordanian television, shortly after Oslo, Arafat explained this strategy: "Since we cannot defeat Israel in war, we do this in stages. We take any and every territory we can of Palestine, and establish sovereignty there, and we use it as a springboard to take more. When the time comes, we can get the Arab nations to join us for the final blow against Israel." That remains Arafat's dream—one shared by the Palestinian people and Arabs throughout the region—to expunge the existence of Israel in stages.

You can have a Jewish state or a Palestinian state. You can not have both.

Why? Consider the topography of Judea and Samaria, designated the West Bank. The Judean mountains are the high ground. (Pre-1967 Israel is a coastal plain.) If Israel controls them, invaders from the East have to fight their way up these heights. In Palestinian hands, Israel's heartland—with 80 percent of its population, most of its industry and military assets—would be within range of mortars, Katyusha rockets and shoulder-held Stinger missiles. Every plane taking off from Tel Aviv's Ben Gurion Airport would become a target. Jerusalem would be surrounded on three sides by hostile territory.

A Terrorist State

Do those in the free world calling for a Palestinian state really want unlimited sovereignty for the Palestinians? Do they really want to have a Palestinian state with its own army, free to dispatch suicide bombers all over the world? Certainly not.

But unlimited sovereignty will produce just that: a fanatical, dictatorial, armed terrorist state in the heart of the Middle East. This state will threaten Israel, America and the entire free world. It will become a university for suicide bombers with departments for every terror organization imaginable—from Hamas to Hezbollah to al Qaeda.

Benjamin Netanyahu, *Betar-Tagar*, July 3, 2003, www.betar.co.uk.

If it loses the land West of the Jordan, instead of an Eastern border 40 miles in length, Israel's new border will be over 200 miles long, impossible to police.

A nation needs strategic depth to survive a surprise attack. The redrawn map of Israel will be nine-miles wide at its narrow waist. A tank column could race across it, and cut the country in half, in short order.

In the decade since Oslo, Arafat has consistently violated his pledges regarding the size of his "police force" and weapons. Even with Israel controlling the borders of the Palestinian Authority, it's proven difficult to block the importation of arms. The *Karine A*, Arafat's illegal arms ship seized in the Red Sea in January, 2002, contained 50 tons of Iranian weapons, including Katyusha rockets, anti-tank missiles, land mines, sniper rifles, mortar shells and explosives. With the Jordanian and Egyptian borders in the hands of a sovereign Palestinian state, weapons—including tanks and anti-aircraft guns—would pour into the Republic of Jihad.

A Palestinian state in the West Bank and Gaza would become a staging area for the conquest of the rest of "Palestine." In the next war, troops and armored columns from Syria and other Arab combatants would have unimpeded access through Palestine to the rump Israeli state.

In an article in the December 1999 issue of *Commentary*, Yuval Steinitz, a member of the Knesset for the Likud party, notes that once the disputed territories have been severed from the rest of the nation, "the tiny area of the Jewish state, together with its over-reliance on reserve forces . . . casts a giant shadow of doubt of another kind altogether: namely, over its ability to withstand a lightning strike. An enemy's penetration into the heart of Israel could prevent the mobilization and equipment of its military reserves in addition to interrupting many other vital operations."

Palestinian forces would be used as an advance column for the main Arab army—infiltrating Israel (across that 200-mile long border), conducting guerrilla operations, disrupting mobilization, cutting supply lines and communications and cause panic in civilian areas.

What amazes me is that—given the record of the "Palestinians," their frequently stated intentions and Israel's geographic vulnerability—anyone in his right mind could imagine that a Palestinian state would exist in peace and harmony with Israel.

President [George W.] Bush says he wants to bring democracy to the Middle East. If he's serious about creating a Palestinian state, he will end up destroying the only democracy in the Middle East—Israel.

The Arab-Moslem Problem

The obstacle to peace in the region isn't the "plight" of the Palestinians or their lack of a state—it's Arab revanchism coupled with Islamic fundamentalism. The idea of a sovereign Jewish state anywhere in the Middle East is intolerable to devout Moslems and Arab nationalists alike—a sacrilege to the former and a mortal affront to the latter.

You will not find a more unlikely candidate for democracy than Arab Moslems. There is a reason why, among the 22 nations of the Arab world, not one even approaches popular rule—why they consistently produce [dictatorial] leaders. . . .

Nor is there a religion less likely to co-exist with other faiths than Islam. From Nigeria, to Egypt, to the Balkans, to Pakistan, the Kashmir and the Philippines, Islam is at war with Christians, Hindus and Jews. The idea that a Palestinian state will be the sole exception to what historian Samuel Huntington calls "Islam's bloody borders" goes beyond wishful thinking.

A Palestinian state would make a mockery of our own war on terror, reward the terror masters and create another Iraq on the borders of our only reliable ally in the region. The only peace it would bring to Israel is the peace of the grave.

"Palestinian propaganda tries to make the fence the issue, and ignores the issue of terrorism which makes the fence necessary."

The Security Fence Between Israel and the Palestinians Is Necessary for Peace

Uzi Landau

Uzi Landau has been a member of the Israeli Knesset since 1984 and served as minister of internal security. In the following viewpoint he argues that the Palestinians have signed agreements with Israel in which they promise to stop terrorism, but they have failed to do so. Therefore, he contends, the only way to prevent Arab terrorists from killing innocent Israelis is to keep them from illegally entering Israel. A security fence, he argues, will promote peace and save lives.

As you read, consider the following questions:
1. How does the author compare Israel's fence to the one on the border between Mexico and the United States?
2. According to the author, how can Palestinian complaints about the fence be resolved?
3. According to Landau, how does the fence promote peace?

When I became Minister of Internal Security [in Israel's government] three years ago, I issued two policy directives to Israel's police. The first was to change our approach to Jerusalem, to stop Palestinian excavations on the Temple Mount, and to change the way Israel dealt with a variety of security apparatuses of the Palestinian Authority that were active in Jerusalem.

The second directive was to prepare staff work for a separation zone between Israel and Judea, Samaria, and Gaza. This separation zone had two objectives: first, to help stop the suicide bombers and the ongoing infiltration from Judea and Samaria into the population centers of Israel; second, to stop the ongoing flow of tens of thousands of illegal Arab immigrants from Judea and Samaria into Israel. When the issue came before the government, it ended up as the security fence plan, and Israel's police were already prepared for it.

The decision to build this barrier was the result of a major shift in Israeli thinking. I was against such a fence and against such a separation for many years. But after 35 years of living with the Palestinians and facing this blatant, ugly, terrorist wave, Israel had no choice but to put up a barrier as an important element in an overall defensive system that would intercept those on their way to blow themselves up among us. Israel has decided to build the security fence because we are in a war that the Palestinians have launched against us, and we have to minimize our casualties.

Israel is now building the fence in Samaria, and we will continue to do so between the mountains of Judea and our southern coastal plain because 130 suicide bombers crossed over from these areas. Only three suicide bombers have come from Gaza where there is already a security fence. Two of them, British citizens, crossed through the gate as tourists.

It is quite clear why the Palestinians are raising hell about the security fence. First of all, they are not interested in peace. They wish to continue and promote terrorism in order to get closer to achieving their political objectives, as they have been doing for the past decades, and in particular over the past decade since [the Oslo peace accords] w[ere] signed. Those who want to have peace want to see the fence, because a precondition to peace is no terrorism.

We are sometimes asked: "Can't you build the fence on the 'green line'? Why should you go into Palestinian areas?" My answer is that we are building it in our own areas. Judea and Samaria is ours. That is our homeland. The Palestinians don't like it. They say it is theirs. Fine, let's sit and negotiate. There is a dispute over this? What do people throughout the world do? They sit and they negotiate.

The Palestinian Future Could Have Been Different

The negotiations between us and the Palestinians through-out our history have been just one-way. The Palestinians extracted all of the concessions, but they have not fulfilled any significant commitments.

They could have had a state after the UN [United Nations] partition resolution in 1947, but they rejected it and launched a war. Between 1947 and 1967 there was no claim for a Palestinian state; nobody had even a hint about the existence of a Palestinian nation, and Israel had no settlements in Judea and Samaria. But Judea and Samaria were used as bases for terrorist activities against Israel proper. The 1967 war started because there was a belief on the part of the Palestinians, the Jordanians, the Egyptians, and the Syrians that from those borders they could easily destroy Israel—borders termed by former foreign minister Abba Eban as "Auschwitz borders." Only after 1967 did the Palestinians start to make their demand for a Palestinian state and start to speak about occupation. Yet when they speak among themselves about occupation, they speak about Israel occupying Tel Aviv and Haifa, not Judea and Samaria.

The Palestinians could have negotiated a different future for themselves in 1978 after the first Camp David [peace treaty] signed between Israel, Egypt, and President [Jimmy] Carter. After a transition period of five years they could have negotiated their future. It didn't take place, of course, because they rejected Camp David. Then in Oslo they signed a peace agreement with Israel. Obviously this would have led them to a state of their own. Yet after grabbing all the concessions, and after Israel had turned over control of all aspects of civilian life for over 97 percent of the Palestinian population, they started a new wave of terrorism.

When former prime minister, [Ehud] Barak met with the Palestinians in 2000 at Camp David, he offered them unprecedented concessions. But these talks were followed by an extreme wave of terrorism that Israel is still fighting today.

Making Israel Safer

The security fence is partially complete and is already producing positive results. In those parts of Israel now protected by the fence, we have experienced a dramatic reduction in terrorist infiltrations. The city of Hadera is a key example. Situated in the heart of Israel, Hadera and its surroundings have suffered a significant series of murderous suicide bombings coming from the West Bank against public transportation centers and shopping malls, resulting in horrific casualties. But since the construction began on the northern sector of the security fence, which shields the region of Hadera, there has been a substantial period of tranquility. This same improvement is true for other Israeli cities and communities now safeguarded by the fence. Can anyone seriously argue against the position that the security fence is making Israeli citizens safer?

Daniel Ayalon, *Washington Times*, August 26, 2003.

Last year [2002] the "Roadmap" [two-state] agreement was presented, in which the Palestinians also had to fulfill a number of commitments, the first and most important of which is putting an end to terrorism. It is tragic that when the Palestinians have the opportunity to negotiate a solution in which they will have the dignity of a state, they refuse to do so unless that state is going to be built on the ruins of the State of Israel. We are not prepared to agree to this.

The terrorists have learned that terrorism pays. They can sign whatever agreements they wish and it really doesn't matter because they will not be made to carry out their commitments, and they can simply carry on with terrorism. Building the fence is to help protect us from that. The route of the fence is determined in part by following the best route that will keep most of the Israelis on one side of the fence. If the Palestinians have any complaints about it, they can blame themselves—Hamas, Islamic Jihad, Tanzim, the

PLO [Palestine Liberation Organization], and [Palestinian Authority leader Yasir] Arafat himself. The fence wasn't there for 35 years; it is there now.

The Issue Is Terrorism, Not the Fence

Palestinian propaganda tries to make the fence the issue, and ignores the issue of terrorism which makes the fence necessary. If not for Palestinian terrorism, we would not need the fence in the first place. They also speak of "walls," even though the segments of wall comprise about 4 percent of the barrier and were built on the "green line," the pre-1967 armistice line, next to Tulkarm and Kalkilya because, in the past, Palestinians have fired from those areas on Israeli vehicles.

There exists a huge fence and walls along long segments of the border between the United States and Mexico, a fence meant to stop people who come to find jobs in the U.S. It takes a lot of audacity to come and demand of us not to have a fence, when we have this fence to intercept those who come to commit mass murder.

We are sorry that some Palestinian families are cut off from their fields. We have tried to provide a reasonable solution for this: providing gates throughout the length of the fence. But even with these gates, there will be inconvenience for certain families. We had to weigh this inconvenience against seeing Israeli families blown to bits if the fence is not built. Faced with these two alternatives, which is morally more compelling?

How the Fence Promotes Peace

But the importance of the fence is not only that it is saving a lot of lives. It is also changing the strategic equation between Israel and terrorism.

The fence will not be any obstacle to future negotiations. If we agree that the separation line will be elsewhere, we will simply move the fence. And in the future if there will be a real peace, why do we need such a fence in the first place? It could be a simpler barrier as you might have between two neighboring countries.

The rights of Jews who live on the other side of the fence will also be negotiated. I take it they will continue to be Israeli citizens, and all of the settlements will continue to be Israeli locales. Jews living in Judea and Samaria are not a barrier to peace. It is absolutely natural that over one million Arabs live within Israel today. For those who say Jews cannot live in Judea and Samaria, the immediate conclusion is that Arabs cannot live in Israel. I think they can, and the symmetry should be kept.

Prime Minister Abu Ala has problems with the fence's location, but the easiest way to get around these problems would be to sit with us and negotiate. The Palestinians made a commitment to dismantle terrorist organizations when they adopted the Roadmap. After signing the agreement, Israel transferred lots of money to the Palestinians, we released prisoners, we withdrew our forces from Bethlehem and from some parts of Gaza. But the Palestinians said they are not going to dismantle the terrorist organizations.

The Palestinians also agreed to entirely stop the incitement that takes place on Palestinian TV, in the media, and in the school system. Right after the Oslo agreement was signed in 1993, Israel's minister of education changed the curriculum and declared the "Year of Peace" in Israeli schools. We taught every child, from elementary school to high school, that the Palestinians were no longer an enemy, they were neighbors. We taught our children that Arafat was no longer a terrorist, he was a partner. By contrast, the Palestinians issued textbooks which taught that Israel is the enemy of mankind, that Jews are Satan on earth, that we are poisoning their wells, and that they should be prepared to become suicide bombers. Today we see the products of that educational system, as the majority of suicide bombers are between the ages of 16 and 28.

"*Officially, Israel argues that the wall is being constructed for security reasons, but the structure's meandering path betrays underlying territorial ambitions.*"

The Security Fence Between Israel and the Palestinians Undermines Peace Efforts

Catherine Cook

In the following viewpoint, Catherine Cook argues that because Israel's security fence encroaches on Palestinian territory, its purpose is not security but the annexation of land. Moreover, the wall, she states, is separating Palestinian farmers from their water and fruit trees, creating great economic hardship. Although Israel claims that the wall is not necessarily permanent, Cook believes that the extreme cost of the project proves that the wall will never be removed. Catherine Cook is media coordinator of the Middle East Research and Information Project.

As you read, consider the following questions:
1. How does Cook describe Israel's separation fence?
2. According to the author, on which side of the separation wall are most Israeli settlements in the occupied territories?
3. According to the author, how does the wall impact Palestinian refugees?

Catherine Cook, "Final Status in the Shape of a Wall," www.merip.org, September 3, 2003. Copyright © 2003 by Catherine Cook. Reproduced by permission.

In Jayyous, a village of 3000 inhabitants in the northern West Bank, Najah Shamasneh cradles her granddaughter in her lap and listens to her husband Yusuf tell of the loss of their agricultural land. The Shamasneh family's 25 dunams (about 2.5 hectares)—their sole source of income—now lies on the western side of the wall that Israel is erecting in the West Bank.

Around the city of Qalqilya, Israel's "security fence" is a 7.6-metre concrete wall crowned by watchtowers at regular intervals. In other areas, such as near the village of Falamiyya, it is a complex arrangement of structures that together form a formidable barrier.

The "fence" begins in the east with a tangle of concertina wire in front of a trench between 2- and 4-metres deep. Behind the trench runs an unpaved military road, a chain link fence topped by barbed wire and then a paved military road. According to reports, the fence is electrified in some places. Combined, these structures stretch across 60 to 100 metres. In some places, a second barbed wire fence bristles on the western side of the paved road. In others, the entirety of the barrier consists of one military road and a barbed wire fence. Thermal imaging cameras, radar-equipped observation towers and touch-sensitive pads have been installed, or soon will be, along much of the wall.

Territorial Ambitions

Officially, Israel argues that the wall is being constructed for security reasons, but the structure's meandering path betrays underlying territorial ambitions. In places, the barrier dips almost 5kms into the West Bank, leaving settlements, fertile Palestinian land and valuable water resources on the "Israeli" side. While the form of the wall varies, everywhere its impact is to confiscate more Palestinian land, isolate Palestinian communities from one another and sap their social and economic viability. This much is well-documented.

Less heavily reported are the links between the wall's humanitarian consequences and political developments. Though the wall is not mentioned in the US-sponsored "road map to peace" [which proposes a new Palestinian state], it intrudes upon each of the main issues to be negotiated during its final phase—the status of Israeli settlements and Jerusalem, the borders between Israel and Palestine, and the fate of Palestinian refugees.

According to Abdullatif Khaled, a hydrologist with the Palestinian Hydrology Group and regional coordinator of the Apartheid Wall Campaign, survey markers first appeared on Jayyous lands in July 2002. Two months later, a resident found affixed to a tree an edict from the Israeli military commander calling the village together to tour the projected route of construction. At the meeting, villages learned that a 5.6km-wide swath—75% of their farmland, thousands of fruit and citrus trees, more than 150 greenhouses and at least six wells—would disappear behind the barrier.

At least an additional 550 dunams [1,000 square meters] were eventually bulldozed to make room for the wall itself, along with another 8000 fruit and citrus trees. With 95% of village's families dependent on the lands behind the wall for their livelihood, the economy of Jayyous has been dealt a serious blow.

Since November 2002, Najah Shamasneh and her family have been living in fields that are now isolated on the "Israeli" side of the apartheid wall. A single gate, controlled by Israel, regulates movement of Palestinian farmers in and out of the fields. According to Khaled, around 300 families travel through the gate on a regular basis. The Shamasnehs, along with 30 or 40 other families, have taken up full-time residence in the area, battling the flies, dirt and summer heat in makeshift shelters. Israel's arbitrary control of the gate makes it impossible for them to tend their crops while living in their family home in the village. Others fear that if they do not maintain a constant presence, at some point they will not be allowed to return.

The main water resources of Jayyous also lie in the area behind the fence. Following Israel's occupation in 1967, according to Khaled, villagers were prohibited from installing pipes to connect the village with the wells in the fields, forcing residents to rely on water tankers. Dependence on transported water and restricted access to the wells have created a serious water deficiency. Last summer [2002], Jayyous had running tap water for only two hours every three days, prompting many villagers to warn of potential health risks.

The Path of the Wall

In late July [2003], Israel's government announced that it had completed the first phase of the construction of the wall in the West Bank. The largest completed section runs from east of Jenin to the settlement of Elkana, south-east of Qalqilya. Smaller segments run from east to west, south of Ramallah and on the northern edge of Bethlehem. In addition, a north-south segment has been built on the eastern edge of Jerusalem. Fourteen gates provide controlled access to agricultural areas on the western side of the wall.

The exact path of the remaining portions of the wall is not yet known. In March, the Israel-based human rights organisation B'tselem reported that while Israel's cabinet had approved the construction of the wall in principle in June 2002, it left authority over its route in the hands of the prime minister and the minister of defence. A variety of proposals are currently under consideration, and a number of factors, including domestic and international opinion, will undoubtedly influence the eventual reach of the barrier.

Unlawful Annexation

The time has come to condemn the wall as an act of unlawful annexation in the language of [UN] Security Council Resolutions 478 and 497, which declare that Israel's actions aimed at the annexation of East Jerusalem and the Golan Heights are "null and void" and should not be recognized by states. Israel's claim that the wall is designed as a security measure with no ulterior motive is simply not supported by the facts.

John Dugard, *International Herald Tribune*, August 2, 2003.

In the meantime, Israeli, Palestinian and international organisations tracking the construction have relied on land confiscation and demolition orders issued to Palestinians, published maps, official statements and satellite imagery to forecast a number of scenarios for the wall's final contours.

Original projections for the western portion were altered in early 2003, when the Israeli defence ministry announced that the wall should extend westward to encompass the Israeli settlements of Ariel and Immanuel, deep in the heart of the West Bank—a position which Prime Minister Ariel Sharon publicly supported. In March, Sharon proclaimed his intention to build another segment of the wall on the western rim of the Jordan Valley.

The wall is projected to have at least three "depth barriers" that will have only one entry/exit point. Outside the walled areas are numerous "enclaves"—pockets of isolated Palestinians—some of which are to be encircled with fences of their own. According to the Palestinian Environmental NGOs [nongovernmental organizations] Network (PENGON), six fenced enclaves will probably be established.

Annexation

If implemented in full, the apartheid wall will confine the majority of the Palestinian population of the West Bank to two or three large cantons (or, more accurately, bantustans like those created by apartheid-era South Africa), comprising some 45 to 50% of the West Bank's territory. If not in these major cantons, Palestinians will be isolated from each other in the "depth barriers", the "enclaves" or in East Jerusalem. "Tunnels" or fenced roads have been proposed to link the cantons.

PENGON estimates that the completed fence will be significantly longer than the Green Line—the 300km-long internationally recognised border between Israel and the West Bank. Construction of the eastern side of the fence would bring the total length of the wall to between 580 and 700kms.

Independent analysts from PENGON, B'tselem and other groups predict that large tracts of land lying outside the wall may eventually be annexed to Israel, but even if not, Israeli regulation of all entry and exit points to Palestinian areas will ensure ultimate Israeli control of the cantons and enclaves. Combined with existing Israeli settlements and the network of settler-only bypass roads developed during the 1990s, Israel's apartheid wall will cement a topography of Palestinian population centres, cut off from one another and from their sources of livelihood.

One of the biggest objections to the wall, voiced by both the Israeli right wing and the US government, has been that Israel is in fact constructing the border of the future Palestinian state. Israel argues that the wall is a temporary security measure, rather than a political *fait accompli.*

However, at an estimated cost of US$2.27 million per kilometre during one of the country's worst economic recessions, claims that the wall is "temporary" appear spurious at best. As UN [United Nations] Special Rapporteur John Dugard noted in the *International Herald Tribune* on August 4 [2003]: "What we are presently witnessing in the West Bank is a visible and clear act of territorial annexation under the guise of security."

The logic behind the snaking route of the barrier can be found in Israel's policies of settlement construction, expropriation of land and the network of bypass roads crisscrossing Palestinian territory. By carefully tailoring the path of the wall to place existing settlements on the "Israeli" side, Israel can maintain control over much of the land, resources, the population and economy of the West Bank. Particularly telling is the fact that projections of the final path of the wall coincide quite closely with Israel's settlement plans dating back decades, especially those favoured by [Israeli Prime Minister] Sharon.

Confiscation and Settlement

For Jayyous residents, the confiscation of their land for the wall is part of a larger pattern of confiscation and settlement dating back to the mid-1980s. Residents report that in 1986, Israel confiscated 1362 dunams of land on which the Israeli settlement of Zofin and a quarry were built. In 1990, Israel confiscated another 30 dunams of land near the eastern entrance to the village and established a rubbish tip for the Israeli settlements.

During the first phase of construction, settler lobbyists succeeded in altering the wall's path to include the Alfe Menashe settlement, which now lies on the western side of the wall. Alfe Menashe (population 5000) now stands within a bubble of territory equivalent in size to the area remaining for Qalqilya (population 42,000). With the resulting uninterrupted territorial contiguity between the settlement and Israel, the future growth of this settlement can be guaranteed.

In contrast, the future of Qalqilya, which is now surrounded on all sides by 8 metres of concrete, seems bleak at best. Entry and exit to the city is regulated by one Israeli army checkpoint. Qalqilya residents have been cut off from surrounding agricultural land and the 32 surrounding villages have been isolated from what was once the commercial centre of the region.

According to B'tselem, Israel built the wall north of the Palestinian villages of Habla, Izbat Jal'ud and Ras Atiyya in order to provide a corridor of direct access from Alfe Menashe to Israel. Residents of Habla must now travel almost 20kms around the wall and through checkpoints to reach Qalqilya, a city that lies 1.6kms away as the crow flies. The Palestinian villages of Ras Atira and al Dab'a, which are near Alfe Menashe, are trapped between the wall and the Green Line, their residents cut off from the West Bank and unable to enter Israel.

Further south, in the Jerusalem area, the first phase of the wall's construction solidified what is widely referred to as the "Jerusalem envelope". The new barriers extending east-west from Ofer military camp to Jaba village (north of Jerusalem) and from Gilo settlement to Umm al Qassis (northeast of Bethlehem), as well as a north-south wall in East Jerusalem, seal off the eastern portion of Jerusalem from the West Bank. Settlements already surround the eastern portion of the city.

To date, the "security fence" places 10 Israeli settlements and approximately 20,000 settlers to its west. With settler groups lobbying to include more major settlements, such as Ariel and Immanuel, on the western side of the wall, and settlements like Shilo and Elon Moreh on the eastern side of the Jordan Valley wall, PENGON projections indicate that 98% of the settler population will be located outside of the wall. Israel is creating "facts on the ground" that will prejudice the outcome of the negotiations over the fate of settlements that are called for in the "road map".

"Final Status" Negotiations

Despite near universal international agreement that Israel's settlements in the Occupied Territories are illegal and constitute a violation of Israel's obligations under the Geneva Convention, their construction has continued unabated, under both Labor and Likud governments, since the 1970s.

While the issue of the settlements was slated for talks during the final status phase of the Oslo process in the 1990s, Israel used the intervening years to double the settlement population and create a network of bypass roads that divide Palestinian territory, while connecting settlements with one another and with Israel. The Palestinian leadership is now faced with having to negotiate the status of settlements that did not exist when they initially agreed to negotiate over settlements in the early 1990s. Settlement construction in and around the Jerusalem area has been so intensive that much of the Israeli public finds it inconceivable to discuss dismantling Jerusalem "neighbourhoods" such as Ma'ale Adumim, a massive housing bloc to the east of the city.

The extent to which the settler movement, thus far, has been able to alter the path of the wall to include settlements on the western side, along with ongoing lobbying about its future path, indicates that the settler population, at least, views (or fears) the wall's construction as more than a temporary measure. Should the wall be completed as projected, in all likelihood its contours, rather than Palestinian needs, will determine the outcome of negotiations on borders. Additionally, as the wall's path becomes clearer, so too does Israel's position on which settlements will remain and which ones are likely to be dismantled.

In effect, Israel is now conducting its own "final status" negotiations—between the Israeli government, the Israeli public and the settler movement. Should the wall be completed, the issues of borders and settlements could be largely decided; the fate of Jerusalem could also be determined, as the city is already enclosed on three sides by settlements and bordered by Israel to the west.

The wall also severely limits options for Palestinian refugees, particularly those forced from their homes in 1948. Since Israel has repeatedly stated that it will allow no refugees to return to homes inside Israel, many analysts have assumed that the bulk of refugees who leave their present abodes will eventually be absorbed within the future Palestinian state. However, if that state will comprise only 45 to 50% of the West Bank, a large-scale resettlement of refugees is doubtful.

In July 2000, Israeli-Palestinian negotiations broke down at Camp David when Palestinian negotiators rejected Israel's "generous offer" that would not have created a contiguous, viable Palestinian state in the West Bank and Gaza Strip. The proposal divided the West Bank into three large cantons, surrounded on all sides, and consequently controlled, by Israeli territory. Completion of all portions of Israel's wall will constitute de facto implementation of the Camp David proposal—but with less territory for the Palestinians.

Economic and Social Impact

Completion of the wall will likely impede the development of an integrated Palestinian economy, leading to further impoverishment, higher unemployment and ruptures in the already strained social fabric. Access to existing jobs, education facilities and health services will be further restricted.

If present plans are followed, not only will Jerusalem be completely separated from the West Bank and, consequently, political, economic and social ties severed, but the physical barriers erected around the city will prevent the Palestinian population there from building outward. The resulting increase in population density, coupled with the wall's hindrance of commerce and investment, could turn much of Jerusalem and other Palestinian towns into urban slums. "Without land, without water, how will people live?", asks PENGON coordinator Jamal Juma.

In Qalqilya, once the urban hub for 32 villages, the effects of the wall are already plain to see. The wall's sealing off of the city has accelerated the economic downturn caused by repeated closures and curfews during the current *intifada* [uprising]. Six hundred out of 1800 shops have closed due to lack of business; the unemployment rate has reached 80%.

In a process of "quiet transfer", as many as 4000 residents have left town in hopes of brighter prospects elsewhere. The heads of an additional 2000 households have been forced to move outside the city to find employment. In Nazlet Issa, north of Tulkarm, construction of the wall has meant the total destruction of its market. In January [2003], the Israeli military destroyed more than 80 of the market's shops. On August 22 [2003], the military completed the job, destroying an additional 100 shops and five houses.

Should the construction of the apartheid wall proceed as planned, similar effects can be expected in other Palestinian communities, adding to the already deep frustrations of Palestinians. Israel's "security fence" could very well lead to greater insecurity and the continuation of conflict.

Periodical Bibliography

The following articles have been selected to supplement the diverse views presented in this chapter.

David Aikman	"Is Peace Possible in the Middle East?" *World & I*, March 2001.
APS Diplomatic News Service	"Arab-Israeli War Is Unavoidable, as Clients Won't Liquidate the 'Terrorist Groups,'" July 7, 2003.
Shlomo Avineri	"Irreconcilable Differences: The Best Solution to the Israeli-Palestinian Conflict Might Be No Solution at All," *Foreign Policy*, March 2002.
Mubarak E. Awad	"The Road to Arab-Israeli Peace," *Tikkun*, January 2001.
Louis Rene Beres	"A Palestinian State and Regional Nuclear War," *Israel Insider*, October 15, 2001.
Avraham Burg	"Arabs and Israelis Must Compromise Their Dreams," *Guardian*, October 10, 2003.
Emuna Elon	"A Fake Palestinian State or a Real One?" *Jerusalem Report*, June 16, 2003.
Don Feder	"Would Palestinian Statehood Be the Beginning of the End for Israel?" *Insight on the News*, July 22, 2002.
Yossi Klein Halevi	"How Despair Is Transforming Israel: The Wall," *New Republic*, July 8, 2002.
Daniel Lazare	"The One-State Solution: However Utopian, Binationalism May Be the Last Hope for Israeli-Palestinian Peace," *Nation*, November 3, 2003.
Ilana Mercer	"Arafat: A Man of the People," *WorldNetDaily*, April 10, 2002.
Melanie Phillips	"Road Map to Hell," *Spectator*, May 17, 2003.
Daniel Pipes	"Arabs Still Want to Destroy Israel," *Wall Street Journal*, January 18, 2002.
Jeffrey Rubinoff	"They Just Do Not Want It," www.MichNews.com, February 26, 2004.
Alain Epp Weaver	"Planned Obsolescence," *Christian Century*, May 3, 2003.
Sherwin Wine	"Arabs and Jews: Is There Any Light at the End of the Tunnel for Peace in the Middle East?" *Humanist*, September/October 2002.

CHAPTER 4

What Should U.S. Policy Be Toward Israel?

Chapter Preface

America's relationship with Israel is often described as "the special relationship." Indeed, it is unique in America's foreign policy. America has been Israel's primary financial and political supporter, having provided approximately $90 billion in economic and military aid to the Jewish state since Israel's creation in 1948. In addition, America nearly always sides with Israel in disputes at the United Nations (UN). The special relationship began when the United States became the first nation to recognize Israel.

The United States did not play a significant role in the events leading up to the formation of the state of Israel because it was not yet a dominant power. When the Zionist movement gathered momentum in the late nineteenth century, the area known as Palestine was ruled by the Ottoman Turks. In 1917, Britain, which was then the leading global power, issued a statement endorsing the creation of a Jewish homeland in Palestine. This statement, known as the Balfour Declaration, was ratified by the League of Nations after World War I. In 1922 the league granted Britain authority (the British Mandate) over Palestine. President Woodrow Wilson expressed agreement with the Balfour Declaration, as did his next three successors: William Harding, Calvin Coolidge, and Herbert Hoover.

During World War II, however, President Franklin Roosevelt took no official position on the creation of a Jewish state in Palestine. Not wanting to alienate the Arabs, whose oil the United States desperately needed, Roosevelt promised that he would consult with both Arabs and Jews before taking a stand on the issue. During the war, defeating the Axis powers was a higher priority than the creation of a Jewish state.

America's position on the issue became crucial after World War II, when it emerged as the leading military and economic power in the world. Unlike President Roosevelt, when Harry S. Truman assumed the presidency, he was openly supportive of the Zionist cause and accepted the Balfour Declaration, which was opposed by both the state and war departments because of fears of disruption in the oil

155

supply. In fact, Truman's secretary of state, the revered former general George Marshall, told Truman he would vote against him in the next election if the president quickly recognized a Jewish state.

The establishment of a Jewish homeland took on added urgency in light of the Holocaust. Britain, eager to rid itself of responsibility for Palestine, which was increasingly consumed by Arab-Jewish fighting, asked the United Nations to intervene. Consequently, on November 29, 1947, the United Nations voted to partition Palestine into two countries—one Arab and one Jewish. This vote was rejected by Palestinian Arabs but welcomed by the Jews. With the withdrawal of the British, there was now a power vacuum in Palestine.

On May 14, 1948, the day the British Mandate over Palestine expired, the Jewish People's Council gathered at the Tel Aviv Museum and approved a proclamation, declaring the establishment of the state of Israel. Eleven minutes after David Ben-Gurion, Israel's first prime minister, read a declaration of independence, the White House issued the following statement: "This government has been informed that a Jewish state has been proclaimed in Palestine, and recognition has been requested by the provisional government thereof. The United States recognizes the provisional government as the de facto authority of the State of Israel." President Truman would later say that his solitary decision to recognize the fledgling state was one of the most difficult he had to make. Truman was guided by his own personal conviction that the creation of Israel was a moral necessity and was consistent with the principle of self-determination.

With the prestige of the United States behind it, the new state of Israel was born, and the "special relationship" had begun. The following viewpoints reflect the great diversity of views regarding America's relationship with Israel.

"All of us, then, should support Israel—all of us, that is, who believe in a world ruled by law and respectful of individual freedom."

The United States Should Support Israel

Bruce S. Thornton

In the following viewpoint, Bruce S. Thornton argues that the United States should support Israel because it is the only liberal democracy in the Middle East. He also claims that Israel is the victim, not the aggressor, in the Arab-Israeli conflict, and therefore deserves our moral support. Finally, he argues that it is in the national interest of the United States to support Israel because democracies such as Israel's promote worldwide peace and stability. Bruce S. Thornton is a professor of classics at California State University Fresno and author of *Bonfire of the Humanities* and *Greek Ways*.

As you read, consider the following questions:
1. According to the author, what has been the impact of the Oslo peace accords?
2. How does Israel fit into the war on terrorism, according to the author?
3. In Thornton's view, what should be our relationship with Saudi Arabia?

Bruce S. Thornton, "Why America Must Support Israel," www.frontpagemag.com, June 14, 2002. Copyright © 2002 by the Center for the Study of Popular Culture. Reproduced by permission.

Tell people you support Israel and they often assume that you're either Jewish or a fundamentalist Christian monitoring Israel's starring role in the drama of Apocalypse. As important as ethnic or religious solidarity is, though, supporting Israel is more firmly based on principle, morality, and national interest.

A Western Society

Principle. Israel is a Western society, like ours the heir of Athens and Jerusalem. This means it is a liberal democracy organized politically to protect the rights of individuals and ensure their participation as citizens in the running of the state. Protecting the freedom of the individual person as a *person*—not as the member of a category—is the primary aim of such a government.

Other features of such a society include: an economic system run to some extent on free-market principles; civilian control of the military; free speech; equality between the sexes; a circumscribed role for religion in government; and a generally secular, rationalist outlook that prizes tolerance and openness rather than the blinkered narrowness of the tribe, clan, or sect. In short, like America Israel is a society of laws rather than powerful men—whether thugs, priests, princes, or bureaucrats—who monopolize force and run society for their own benefit.

This is the ideal, one that no society, Israel or our own, perfectly realizes. Yet considering that Israel has since its birth lived besieged by incessant aggression against its very existence, the issue is not that Israel compromises on some of these principles in order to survive, but rather that it embodies *any* of them. An Israeli Arab member of parliament can rise up in the Knesset and publicly criticize the Prime Minister, something he could not do in any other Arab state, at least if he wanted to stay out of jail or survive the night.

As the only liberal democracy in the whole Middle East, then, Israel demands our support—*if* we believe in the principle, as we say we do, that such a society is the best way for people to live, no matter what their race, national origin, or religion, for it maximizes the freedom and prosperity of the greatest number of individuals.

Victim, Not Aggressor

Morality. Despite the media's rhetoric of moral equivalence (often the last refuge of the morally bankrupt), there is a clear right and a wrong in this conflict. If we cut through the fog of "checkpoints" and "settlements," we can see clearly the source of the conflict: the Arab attempt to destroy Israel. Does anyone really think that if the Arabs had sincerely accepted Israel in 1948 that the subsequent fifty years would have been as bloody and miserable as they have been for both sides? Quite simply, Israel kills Palestinians and restricts their movements because for fifty years Palestinians have murdered Israelis, egged on by Islamic nations whose populations outnumber Israel 100 to one.

Thus whatever Israel's mistakes or injustices, they have been the byproducts of Israel's attempt to defend its very existence against a sustained, fifty-year assault by terror, guerilla action, and three wholesale military attacks. And whatever the Palestinians have suffered has its ultimate origins in the existence of a critical mass of Arabs who do not accept Israel's right to live and hence compel Israel to defend itself, with all the tragic, unforeseen consequences that always accompany even the just use of force.

Natural Allies

America and Israel have a special friendship. In fact, it's more than a friendship. America and Israel are brothers and sisters in the family of democracy, natural allies—natural allies in the cause of peace.

The family of democracy transcends borders and oceans. What unites us is a powerful conviction, perhaps the greatest of all convictions. "We hold these truths to be self-evident, that all men are created equal, that they are endowed by their Creator with certain unalienable rights, that among these are life, liberty, and the pursuit of happiness."

George W. Bush, statement to the American Israel Public Affairs Committee Conference, May 22, 2000.

The old Greeks understood the moral principle very well: "The doer suffers." He who initiates violence and aggression and threatens another's existence will unleash a defensive response and suffer the consequences. I'm not speaking of the media's "cycle of violence," a phrase that obscures moral responsibility, as though Palestinian murder of civilians and the Israeli defensive response are natural phenomena like the seasons. Violence used to defend is morally different from violence used to destroy.

Finally, there is one critical moral distinction that needs to be affirmed: the inadvertent death of civilians resulting from the use of force to defend one's self is utterly and absolutely different from the planned targeting of civilians to destroy another. A man who shoots at your family while hiding behind his own bears all the responsibility if his family is killed when you defend yourself.

Let us state once more the obvious: if Palestinians stop killing Israelis, Palestinians will stop dying. But the reverse is not true: [The failed Oslo peace accords between Israel and the Palestinians have] shown that the more Israel accommodates Palestinian aspirations, the more Israelis who will die.

Defeating Terrorism

National Interest. In the short-term, defending Israel might appear to be contrary to our national interests. After all, there is no oil in Israel, and supporting her annoys those larger, more strategically placed nations who do possess oil. But this way of thinking is dangerously shortsighted.

Our national interests are more easily served and defended the more liberal democracies there are. Societies of free citizens and free markets are more stable and peaceful, and less prone to aggression against their neighbors. Given that there are no genuinely free societies in the Middle East, it is definitely in our national interest to defend and support a trusted and loyal democratic ally, and to work at creating more such democracies in the region. An ally like Saudi Arabia might serve our short-term interests, but its chronic instability and dysfunctional political order is a time bomb that someday will explode in our faces.

More important, though, after [the September 11, 2001, terrorist attacks] we now know that it is very much in our interests to defeat terror, and Israel is the key battleground in the war on terror. Quite simply, if homicide-bombers work in Israel, or even *appear* to be working, then the rest of the world will regularly suffer from such attacks. Those who think terror is a legitimate instrument for achieving their aims must be utterly and thoroughly defeated and convinced that terror will *never* result in anything other than their own destruction.

All of us, then, should support Israel—all of us, that is, who believe in a world ruled by law and respectful of individual freedom. As rare and fragile a plant as such freedom has been in human history, principle, morality, and interest all tell us that we cannot afford to see it uprooted anywhere.

"The old strategic reasons for shoring up Israel were obliterated once and for all when the World Trade Center came tumbling down."

The United States Should Not Support Israel

Sarah Helm

In the following viewpoint, Sarah Helm argues that America's financial, military, and political support for Israel fuels militancy in the Muslim world. In order to maintain an effective coalition in the war against terrorism, she claims, America must end its unqualified support for Israel, which breeds anti-Americanism in the Middle East. Sarah Helm was Jerusalem correspondent for the *Independent* (London).

As you read, consider the following questions:
1. According to the author, what role does the pro-Israel lobby play in American-Israeli relations?
2. What did the September 11, 2001, terrorist attacks prove about our approach to Israel, according to the author?
3. According to the author, what caused the failure of the Camp David peace summit in 2000?

The US always supports Israel at the UN [United Nations] and gives it one-sixth of its entire foreign aid budget.

Before [the September 11, 2001, terrorist attacks] George W. Bush had a very clear policy on the Israel-Palestine conflict—keep out of it. When Bush came to power, Israel's prime minister, Ariel Sharon, was already busy obliterating the last feeble achievements of the Oslo peace process. He was using US-manufactured F-16 aircraft to attack civilian Palestinian targets, and was spending his US dollars on expanding settlements. Meanwhile, Palestinian despair was fuelling support for the second intifada [uprising]. The use of suicide bombers against Israel became an accepted element of the Palestinian weaponry, and showed that the militants in the West Bank and Gaza were winning sympathisers to their cause.

But none of this was a matter for the new Republican president in the United States. As one American foreign policy adviser put it to me in August [2001], just days after a Palestinian suicide bomber had killed 18 Israelis in a Jerusalem pizza restaurant: "The calculation has been made that there is no need to get involved."

Now, we are told, nothing will ever be the same again. And that includes America's relationship with Israel.

In the wake of the World Trade Center disaster, Washington suddenly recognised that the Israel-Palestine conflict is central to its interests. Binding Arab states into the new US-led antiterrorist coalition became a top priority. The Arab leaders said they would support America—but only if pressure was put on Israel to reconsider its position in the peace talks. Bush immediately had words—strong words—with Sharon, telling him to call a truce with the Palestinian leader, Yasser Arafat, and to despatch Shimon Peres to meet Arafat for talks.

In response, Sharon drove his tanks deeper into the West Bank. By Tuesday [September 18, 2001], while Sharon had still not agreed to a truce, Arafat was earning praise in the US for his "100 per cent support" in the wake of the attacks (remember his blood-giving photo-op?) and for his "100 per cent effort" to reduce Palestinian violence. American anger at the Israeli prime minister's intransigence has been palpable. The *Washington Post* even went so far as to point out that Sharon was "endangering" the fight against terrorism. Does this fracas suggest any long-term change in relations between the US and Israel?

The Pro-Israel Lobby

America's relationship with Israel is special in a way that makes its relationship with Britain look like a one-night stand. The common figure given for US aid to Israel is $3bn a year, of which $1.2bn is in the form of economic aid and $1.8bn in the form of military aid. The figure represents a staggering one-sixth of total US foreign aid. Year after year, America's ever-powerful pro-Israel lobby gears up to ensure that the sums are voted through Congress. The money, it has always been argued, is well worth spending to support a valiant Israel, a beacon of democracy and freedom, and a vital ally to the US in a troubled Middle East.

But the relationship is not only about money. In the corridors and voting chambers of the United Nations, the US and Israel are inseparable. Since 1972, half of all UN resolutions on Palestine have been vetoed by the US, including resolutions ordering Israel to stop building illegal Jewish settlements on occupied land and to stop changing the status of the illegally occupied Arab East Jerusalem.

In peace negotiations, the US has stood shoulder to shoulder with Israel whenever the chips were down. Any pretence of honest brokerage during the Camp David peace summit last year [2000] was exposed as being just that—a pretence—when a former White House aide, Robert Malley, admitted in an article published in the *New York Review of Books* that the failure of the talks had been due as much to broken promises by Bill Clinton and Ehud Barak, the former US and Israeli leaders, as to Arafat's refusal to deal.

And now the attacks on the twin towers in New York and the Pentagon in Washington offer an opportunity for the US to rethink its relationship with Israel.

Bush himself has been at pains to stress that the US must not only hit back militarily at the culprits and those regimes that back them, but must also begin to "deal with the pool" in which the terrorists swim. His defence secretary, Donald

Rumsfeld, speaks of "draining the swamp".

Whatever language its leaders choose to use, if they are now serious about transforming the attitudes that lend support to Muslim extremism, they must look long and hard at the stark realities of Israel's illegal occupation, and begin to acknowledge the humiliation and desperation that its daily injustices create.

No Special Relationship

We have no special relationship with Israel. That's more disinformation to hide the fact that our politicians have just sold out. How can you have a special relationship with a country that takes billions of your tax dollars, attacks your Navy ships, blows up your diplomatic facilities and spies on you? Ask yourself: What has Israel ever done for the United States?

Charley Reese, http://reese.king-online.com, May 24, 2002.

[Terrorist leader] Osama Bin Laden did not send his suicide bombers into the World Trade Center because of Palestine. It would be laughable to suggest that he might have called off his attacks had the Oslo peace process still been in place. And yet it is irrefutable that the Palestinian cause, more than any other cause that the Muslim world might seize on, including Iraq, is the one that most swiftly fuels militancy in the Arab world. Anyone who has travelled around the Middle East knows that the role the US plays in underpinning Israel is the prime focus of anti-American sentiment.

Double Standard

The US needs to be able to seize the moral high ground as it builds its coalition against terrorism. Yet how can it preach the values of the free world to a Middle East where more than two million Palestinians are caged within enclaves by an Israeli military machine that is bankrolled by American taxpayers?

How can the US preach about democracy and human rights when more than three million Palestinian refugees are scattered around the world, many in camps, without even the right to return to their homes? And how can the US expect the Muslim world to listen to its condemnation of religious fanaticism without at least paying heed to the policies of Israel that encourage extreme and fanatic Jewish settlers to seize Arab land?

The old strategic reasons for shoring up Israel were obliterated once and for all when the World Trade Center came tumbling down. Any case for building a militarised "fortress Israel" was exposed as futile by Palestinian suicide bombers long before the vulnerability of the US was so savagely exposed. It remains to be seen, however, whether even these seismic events can shift America's most dogged domestic political consensus into rethinking the country's relationship with Israel.

The Republican Party today is packed with right-wing hawks and religious conservatives who are unlikely to see a new tilt towards the Palestinians as anything other than a reward for terrorism. Bush's two right-hand men—the secretary of state, Colin Powell, and the vice-president, Dick Cheney—are both veterans of coalition-building during the Gulf war, when they served under a more internationalist president, George Bush Sr. They may well be urging George Bush Jr to take a tougher stance with Israel. Powell, in particular, has shown signs that he does not wish to be in thrall to the pro-Israel lobby.

Yet even if the president himself can be convinced of the need for a shift away from Israel, it is hard to believe that he could summon the strength to convince his party—still less his people. America is a country that is often less critical of Israel than is Israel itself. Nevertheless, a battle to change American minds must begin: if this opportunity for change is missed, there is little doubt that suicide bombers will continue to spring from the refugee camps of Gaza and the West Bank. There is also little doubt that the wider pool in which the Islamic militancy swims will continue to fill.

*"America suffered 9/11 and its aftermath
. . . mainly because U.S. policy in the
Middle East is made in Israel, not in
Washington."*

America's Support of Israel Led to the September 11 Terrorist Attacks

Paul Findley

Paul Findley contends in the following viewpoint that the September 11, 2001, terrorist attacks on America would not have happened if the United States did not support Israel. According to Findley, the attacks were the result of anti-American sentiment because of U.S. support for Israel. He argues that the United States should suspend all aid to Israel unless it withdraws from the occupied Palestinian territories. Paul Findley was a representative in the U.S. Congress for twenty-two years. He is the author of *They Dare to Speak Out*.

As you read, consider the following questions:
1. According to the author, what is Israel's territorial goal?
2. As argued by Findley, what role does Israel's U.S. lobby play in the creation of America's policy toward Israel?
3. What role does religion play in Israeli politics, according to the author?

[The September 11, 2001, terrorist attacks] would not have occurred if the U.S. government had refused to help Israel humiliate and destroy Palestinian society. Few express this conclusion publicly, but many believe it is the truth. I believe the catastrophe could have been prevented if any U.S. president during the past 35 years had had the courage and wisdom to suspend all U.S. aid until Israel withdrew from the Arab land seized in the 1967 Arab-Israeli war.

The U.S. lobby for Israel is powerful and intimidating, but any determined president—even President [George W.] Bush this very day—could prevail and win overwhelming public support for the suspension of aid by laying these facts before the American people:

Israel's present government, like its predecessors, is determined to annex the West Bank—biblical Judea and Samaria—so Israel will become Greater Israel. Ultra-Orthodox Jews, who maintain a powerful role in Israeli politics, believe the Jewish Messiah will not come until Greater Israel is a reality. Although a minority in Israel, they are committed, aggressive, and influential. Because of deep religious conviction, they are determined to prevent Palestinians from gaining statehood on any part of the West Bank.

In its violent assaults on Palestinians, Israel uses the pretext of eradicating terrorism, but its forces are actually engaged advancing the territorial expansion just cited. Under the guise of anti-terrorism, Israeli forces treat Palestinians worse than cattle. With due process nowhere to be found, hundreds are detained for long periods and most are tortured. Some are assassinated. Homes, orchards, and business places are destroyed. Entire cities are kept under intermittent curfew, some confinements lasting for weeks. Injured or ill Palestinians needing emergency medical care are routinely held at checkpoints for an hour or more. Many children are undernourished. The West Bank and Gaza have become giant concentration camps. None of this could have occurred without U.S. support. Perhaps Israeli officials believe life will become so unbearable that most Palestinians will eventually leave their ancestral homes.

Once beloved worldwide, the U.S. government finds itself reviled in most countries because it provides unconditional support of Israeli violations of the United Nations Charter, international law, and the precepts of all major religious faiths.

How did the American people get into this fix?

Nine-eleven had its principal origin 35 years ago when Israel's U.S. lobby began its unbroken success in stifling debate about the proper U.S. role in the Arab-Israeli conflict and effectively concealed from public awareness the fact that the U.S. government gives massive uncritical support to Israel.

Thanks to the suffocating influence of Israel's U.S. lobby, open discussion of the Arab-Israeli conflict has been nonexistent in our government all these years. I have firsthand knowledge, because I was a member of the House of Representatives Foreign Affairs Committee in June 1967 when Israeli military forces took control of the Golan Heights, a part of Syria, as well as the Palestinian West Bank and Gaza. I continued as a member for 16 years and to this day maintain a close watch on Congress.

No Debate Allowed

For 35 years, not a word has been expressed in that committee or in either chamber of Congress that deserves to be called debate on Middle East policy. No restrictive or limiting amendments on aid to Israel have been offered for 20 years, and none of the few offered in previous years received more than a handful of votes. On Capitol Hill, criticism of Israel, even in private conversation, is all but forbidden, treated as downright unpatriotic, if not anti-Semitic. The continued absence of free speech was assured when those few who spoke out—Senators Adlai Stevenson and Charles Percy, and Reps. Paul "Pete" McCloskey, Cynthia McKinney, Earl Hilliard, and myself—were defeated at the polls by candidates heavily financed by pro-Israel forces.

As a result, legislation dealing with the Middle East has been heavily biased in favor of Israel and against Palestinians and other Arabs year after year. Home constituencies, misled by news coverage equally lop-sided in Israel's favor, remain largely unaware that Congress behaves as if it were a subcommittee of the Israeli parliament.

However, the bias is widely noted beyond America, where

September 11 Has Forever Changed the World

Let us pray for the American victims of [the September 11, 2001, terrorist attacks] and for their suffering families. Let us go after the perpetrators of these dastardly acts with absolute precision.

But, even more importantly, let us understand why these events occurred and how we can heal the hatred against our nation.

Many traitors in our government have supported Zionism's criminal activities rather than the true interests of the American people. They have spawned the hatred against America that drove on these terrible acts. They are as much responsible for the carnage of September 11 as if they themselves piloted these planes that were turned into bombs.

This event happened because the American government and media are ruled by those who put Israel's interests over America's. Unless that foreign power over us is broken, Americans will be haunted by an increasing specter of terrorism.

David Duke, October 8, 2001, www.davidduke.com.

---

most news media candidly cover Israel's conquest and generally excoriate America's complicity and complacency. When President Bush welcomed Israeli Prime Minister Ariel Sharon, sometimes called the Butcher of Beirut, as "my dear friend" and "a man of peace" after Israeli forces, using U.S.-donated arms, completed their devastation of the West Bank last spring [2001], worldwide anger against American policy reached the boiling point.

Arab Fury

The fury should surprise no one who reads foreign newspapers or listens to BBC. In several televised statements long before 9/11, Osama bin Laden, believed by U.S. authorities to have masterminded 9/11, cited U.S. complicity in Israel's destruction of Palestinian society as a principal complaint. Prominent foreigners, in and out of government, express their opposition to U.S. policies with unprecedented frequency and severity, especially since Bush announced his determination to make war against Iraq.

The lobby's intimidation remains pervasive. It seems to

reach every government center and even houses of worship and revered institutions of higher learning. It is highly effective in silencing the many U.S. Jews who object to the lobby's tactics and Israel's brutality.

Nothing can justify 9/11. Those guilty deserve maximum punishment, but it makes sense for America to examine motivations promptly and as carefully as possible. Terrorism almost always arises from deeply-felt grievances. If they can be eradicated or eased, terrorist passions are certain to subside.

Today, a year after 9/11, President Bush has made no attempt to redress grievances, or even to identify them. In fact, he has made the scene far worse by supporting Israel's religious war against Palestinians, an alliance that has intensified anti-American anger. He seems oblivious to the fact that nearly two billion people worldwide regard the plight of Palestinians as today's most important foreign-policy challenge. No one in authority will admit a calamitous reality that is skillfully shielded from the American people but clearly recognized by most of the world: America suffered 9/11 and its aftermath and may soon be at war with Iraq,[1] mainly because U.S. policy in the Middle East is made in Israel, not in Washington.

Israel is a scofflaw nation and should be treated as such. Instead of helping Sharon intensify Palestinian misery, our president should suspend all aid until Israel ends its occupation of Arab land Israel seized in 1967. The suspension would force Sharon's compliance or lead to his removal from office, as the Israeli electorate will not tolerate a prime minister who is at odds with the White House.

If Bush needs an additional reason for doing the right thing, he can justify the suspension as a matter of military necessity, an essential step in winning international support for his war on terrorism. He can cite a worthy precedent When President Abraham Lincoln issued the proclamation that freed only the slaves in states that were then in rebellion, he made the restriction because of "military necessity."

If Bush suspends U.S. aid, he will liberate all Americans from long years of bondage to Israel's misdeeds.

---

1. The United States and a coalition of allies invaded Iraq in March 2003.

"There simply is no correlation between the new terrorism facing the U.S. and the Arab-Israeli peace process."

America's Support of Israel Did Not Lead to the September 11 Terrorist Attacks

Jerusalem Center for Public Affairs

In the following viewpoint, the Jerusalem Center for Public Affairs argues that despite statements to the contrary in the media, America's support for Israel was not the driving force behind the September 11, 2001, terrorist attacks. The center claims that the primary motivation behind September 11 mastermind Osama bin Laden's anger at America was the U.S. troops then stationed in Saudi Arabia. The Jerusalem Center for Public Affairs is a research and public policy advocacy organization concerned with issues related to Israel and Jewish people.

As you read, consider the following questions:
1. According to the center, how was Osama bin Laden's network involved with the Israeli-Palestinian conflict?
2. According to the author, what areas are the main focus of Osama bin Laden's terrorist network?
3. What is the role of the Arab media in creating anti-American sentiment in the Muslim world, in the center's view?

After witnessing the September 11 [2001] terrorist assault on the World Trade Center and the Pentagon, many American analysts have been seeking to understand the source of the intense hatred against the United States that could have motivated an act of violence on such an unprecedented scale. In that context, a new canard is beginning to run through repeated news reports and features: that somehow America's support for Israel is behind the fury of militant Islamic movements, like that of [terrorist] Osama Bin Laden, towards the United States.

Thus, Tony Karon of *Time* (September 14 [2001]) wrote: "the motivation to launch a spectacular attack would have grown exponentially over the past year as anti-American feeling surged in the Arab streets in response [to] U.S. support for Israel" (September 14, http://HonestReporting.com). On September 16, Caryl Murphy of the *Washington Post* states: "If we want to avoid creating more terrorists, we must end the Israeli-Palestinian conflict quickly." Gary Kamya, *Salon* magazine's executive editor, adds similarly: "A sword will hang over the U.S. until we convince Israel to make peace with the Palestinians."

Yet a careful examination of the ideology and organization of Bin Laden's al-Qaida terrorist network demonstrates that these increasingly ubiquitous assertions are seriously flawed. In fact, state-supported media in parts of the Arab world continually engage in incitement of the Arab civilian population against the United States, regardless of the Israeli factor. Unless the sources of anti-Americanism are correctly understood and addressed, policy makers are likely to fail to deal with true motivating factors behind the attack on the United States.

The Ideological Sources of the Anti-Americanism of Bin Laden

A 1998 Fatwa (religious ruling) issued by Bin Laden jointly with militant Islamic leaders from Egypt, Pakistan, and Bangladesh provides an insight into the sources of his anti-Americanism (*Al-Quds Al-Arabi*, Feb. 23, 1998, www.ict.org.il). The document calls "on every Muslim . . . to kill the Americans and plunder their money wherever and whenever they find it." The primary justification for doing so is that "for over seven years the United States has been occupying the lands of Islam in the holiest of places, the Arabian Peninsula, plundering its riches, dictating to its rulers, humiliating its people, [and] terrorizing its neighbors." Having helped to defeat the Soviet Union in Afghanistan in the 1980s with other Arab volunteers, Bin Laden has now turned his attention to the remaining superpower, the United States. U.S. forces are specifically described as "crusader armies spreading . . . like locusts."

A second Bin Laden grievance is "the continuing aggression against the Iraqi people." The "guarantee of Israel's survival" appears only as the third reason for criticizing U.S. policy. And here, Israel's very existence is the issue—not the status of the peace process. It is not surprising that the planning and training for the September 11 attack is believed to have begun several years ago, well before the current Palestinian intifada and the stalemate in the Israeli-Palestinian peace process. There simply is no correlation between the new terrorism facing the U.S. and the Arab-Israeli peace process.

The Organizational Priorities of the Bin Laden Network

An examination of Bin Laden's organization network further reveals that the issue of Israel is not a top priority for his brand of militant Islam. The U.S. Department of State's *Patterns of Global Terrorism—2000* identifies Sunni Islamic extremist groups that have been linked to Osama Bin Laden's worldwide network: the Egyptian Islamic Jihad, Egypt's al-Gama'at al-Islamiyya, the Islamic Movement of Uzbekistan, and the Harakat ul-Mujahidin, a Pakistan-based group operating against India in Kashmir. Additionally, Bin Laden's network is known to reach Albania, the Philippines, Chechnya, Indonesia, Jordan, Lebanon, the former Yugoslavia, Sudan, and Yemen. Their common goals appear to be the overthrow of pro-American regimes in the Middle East and the assertion of Muslim independence in multi-ethnic states.

Reuven Paz of the Herzilya International Policy Institute for Counter Terrorism has noted that the Bin Laden network has not connected with militant Islamic movements in the

West Bank and Gaza Strip, despite its mobilization of Palestinians from Lebanon and Jordan over the last decade (*ICT*, April 24, 2000). The U.S. Department of State noted only one case of a militant, Nabil Awkil, connected to both Hamas and Osama Bin Laden and very few other cases have been identified. This minimal involvement of Bin Laden's network might be due to the fact that the main Palestinian figure who brought other Palestinians to participate in the struggle of militant Islam in Afghanistan, Dr. Abdallah Azam, was killed in 1989 in Pakistan. Other Palestinians might have been attracted to the Iranian model, adopted by Islamic Jihad.

U.S. Support for Israel Did Not Play Much of a Part

In the wake of [the September 11, 2001, terrorist attacks] many argued that we brought the attack upon ourselves because of our support for Israel. Even were this true, we should no more end that support than we should eliminate religious freedom and women's rights in our country—hallmarks of our democracy that also engage the wrath of the terrorists who attacked us. And it beggars belief to think our support for Israel played much of any part for the attack upon us.

William J. Bennett, *National Review Online*, July 22, 2003. www.national review.com.

Still, if the Palestinian issue were a high priority for Bin Laden, then efforts to mobilize Palestinian militants and establish a widespread presence in the territories would have been far more extensive. Instead, the Bin Laden network largely reflects the concerns of an Afghan-based organization with strong links to Pakistan; hence, its involvement in the Indian subcontinent, the former Muslim republics of the Soviet Union, and strategic points around the Arabian Peninsula, especially Yemen.

The Supportive Media Environment in Arab States

One of the surprising aspects of the September [2001] attack on the U.S. is the role of nationals who come from states that are thought to be friendly to the U.S.: Egypt, Saudi Arabia, and the UAE [United Arab Emirates]. However, Bin Laden's anti-Americanism has considerable resonance in the government-controlled media of much of the Arab world. Even Egypt's official media have contributed to this environment. Thus, a columnist in the state-controlled *Al-Akhbar* wrote in August 2001:

> The conflict that we call the Arab-Israeli conflict is, in truth, an Arab conflict with Western, particularly American, colonialism. . . . The U.S. treats the [Arabs] as it treated the slaves inside the American continent. . . . The issue no longer concerns the Israeli-Arab conflict. The real issue is the Arab-American conflict. (*MEMRI*, Analysis No. 71).

Writing less than a month before the attack on the World Trade Center and the Pentagon, the columnist stated that "The Statue of Liberty, in New York Harbor, must be destroyed." Unfortunately, this sort of anti-Americanism is not uncommon.

Placing Israel and the Palestinian issue in the spotlight of the current anti-Americanism motivating the militant Islamic groups connected with Osama Bin Laden is simply wrong. It can also lead to a misplaced emphasis in current U.S. policy options toward the Middle East. In order to address the hostile environment toward the U.S. in parts of the Arab world today, anti-American incitement in government-controlled media should be examined. Eliminating terrorism requires not only purely military measures, but also diplomatic moves aimed at making sure that there is no fertile ground for mobilizing more militant operations. While press-freedoms are to be respected, systematic anti-American incitement of whole populations must cease in order to create an environment that is not supportive of future attacks against the U.S. and its citizens.

"The United States must make a sustained, all-out push for a cessation of violence and a return to serious peace talks."

The United States Should Resolve the Israeli-Palestinian Conflict

Lee H. Hamilton

Lee H. Hamilton argues in the following viewpoint that U.S. intervention is required for any solution to the Israeli-Palestinian conflict. According to Hamilton, all world leaders look to the United States to lead the peace effort. He states that America's security and international standing depend upon a successful peace agreement. Former U.S. congressman Lee H. Hamilton is director of the Woodrow Wilson International Center for Scholars.

As you read, consider the following questions:
1. According to Hamilton, what is the only viable solution to the Israeli-Palestinian conflict?
2. What would result from a failure to resolve the Israeli-Palestinian conflict in the author's view?
3. In Hamilton's opinion, what must Arab nations do to contribute to a resolution to the Israeli-Palestinian conflict?

The escalation of violence between Israel and the Palestinians presents a critical and difficult challenge for American foreign policy. The conflict is threatening to destabilize moderate Arab governments, disrupt global oil supplies, weaken international support for the war on terrorism, and spiral out of control—possibly leading to a broader war in the Middle East. The United States must make a sustained, all-out push for a cessation of violence and a return to serious peace talks.

The two sure things in the Israeli-Palestinian conflict are that it will not be resolved by force and that its resolution requires sustained U.S. intervention. Everyone—from the Israelis and Palestinians to European and Arab leaders—looks to the U.S. to set the agenda and push the parties toward a comprehensive agreement.

Until this month [April 15, 2002], President [George W.] Bush was reluctant to become deeply involved in the conflict because he did not want a major diplomatic initiative to fail. But his recent bold and forward-looking statements, and his dispatching of Secretary of State [Colin] Powell to the region, have placed the U.S. back at the center of efforts to resolve the conflict. Bush has laid out an inspiring vision of Middle East peace, grounded in the end of violence, the establishment of a Palestinian state, and Arab acceptance of Israel. The challenge now is to fill in the details of that vision and get the Israelis, Palestinians, and Arab countries to agree to them.

The U.S. must work with Europe and friendly Arab nations to mobilize international support for a new peace effort that seeks not only to settle the Israeli-Palestinian conflict but also to achieve a broad regional peace between Israel and all of its Arab neighbors. The outlines of a settlement, involving at heart an Israeli withdrawal from the occupied territories in exchange for peace and security, are already fairly clear. As in many policy problems, it is not the destination that is most at issue, but how to get there.

To make progress, a cease-fire must be linked to confidence-building measures and a resumption of peace negotiations—so that Israelis can feel safe and Palestinians and their Arab supporters can have confidence that they are moving towards a viable Palestinian state. The U.S. must press the Israelis and Palestinians to take concrete actions to reduce the violence and develop a measure of trust. The Palestinian leadership must condemn terrorism and extremism in the strongest terms and work with Israel to crack down on terrorist networks. Israel must withdraw its military forces from Palestinian territories, ease restrictions on Palestinian movement, and stop expanding settlements.

The United States Can Help

First, the United States can help end current hostilities and stem the possibility of that violence spilling over into a broader regional war. Instead of merely relying on Israelis and Palestinians to act, the United States could address some root causes of the current dilemma.

Palestinians need to have their hope restored. The United States can help provide that with a clear expression of support for the legitimate Palestinian right to a sovereign state, with a capital in Jerusalem, exercising full control over its own borders. A firm U.S. statement of opposition to Israeli settlements would also be helpful. It should be made clear to the Israelis that they can have settlements or peace, but not both.

James Zogby, *Baltimore Sun*, November 29, 2000.

Once the violence has abated and confidence-building measures have begun, negotiations should aim to reach agreement on the most difficult issues of borders, the future of Jerusalem, and Palestinian refugees. The only viable solution to the conflict is the establishment of two states, Israel and Palestine, living side-by-side in peace and security. Israel will have to withdraw to something close to its pre-1967 borders and dismantle all but a few of its settlements in the West Bank and Gaza. Creative compromises will be necessary (and are possible) to divide control over Jerusalem and its holy sites, and to allow Palestinian refugees to settle in their current countries of residence, in the new state of Palestine, in third countries, or, in small numbers to be agreed upon, in Israel.

Additionally, Arab nations must accept the legitimacy of the Jewish state of Israel and develop normal diplomatic and economic relations with it. Full peace will not come to the

Middle East until Israel feels secure with all of its neighbors. A major peace conference might be necessary to hammer out a broad regional agreement.

Throughout this process, Israeli, Palestinian, and Arab leaders must prepare their people for the compromises necessary to achieve agreements. I do not accept the view that neither [Palestinian leader Yasir] Arafat nor [Israeli prime minister Ariel] Sharon can reach an agreement—either because they are unwilling or incapable of it. Israel and the Palestinians will have to come to an agreement eventually because there is no viable alternative. Israel cannot rule an ever-growing Palestinian population and the Palestinians cannot expel Israel by force.

In light of the horrific violence of recent weeks [around April 15, 2002], talk of a comprehensive settlement to the Israeli-Arab conflict might seem premature. But the failure of terrorism or military assaults to achieve Palestinian or Israeli goals should help all parties understand that there is no military solution to the dispute. The United States must take the lead in bringing the Israelis and Palestinians back from the brink. Our own security and international standing depend on our success in this crucial task.

"No one should expect that a national conflict . . . could be resolved in a week of talks in Camp David. And getting Washington to 'do something' is not going to transform this reality."

The United States Should Not Resolve the Israeli-Palestinian Conflict

Leon Hadar

In the following viewpoint, Leon Hadar argues that the United States should not attempt to mediate between the Israelis and the Palestinians. Hadar contends that previous U.S. involvement in peace talks doomed them to failure. Instead, he suggests that the countries in the region, such as Saudi Arabia, Egypt, and Jordan, should take the lead in bringing a resolution to the conflict. Leon Hadar is a research fellow in foreign policy studies at the Cato Institute and former UN bureau chief at the *Jerusalem Post*.

As you read, consider the following questions:
1. According to Hadar, what resulted from President Bill Clinton's attempts to resolve the Israeli-Palestinian conflict?
2. Which countries does the author believe should provide peacekeeping troops as part of a solution?
3. What role does Hadar believe the European Union should play in a Middle East peace plan?

President [George W.] Bush has stressed the need for America's allies to play the lead role in ending conflicts and maintaining security in their strategic backyards. According to this view, the European Union should shoulder the responsibility for dealing with the civil wars in the Balkans, while the Association of Southeast Asian Nations (ASEAN) and Australia should be responsible for containing ethnic instability in Indonesia.

But while Republican leaders seem ready to shift the burden of maintaining stability in parts of Asia and Europe to allies, they don't seem to want to apply that paradigm to the Israeli-Palestinian conflict. Yet that dispute is the kind of regional problem that can be dealt with by local players whose long-term military, economic and demographic interests are affected by the clashes in the Holy Land.

Clinton's Failure

The disastrous results of the hyperactive American diplomacy under President [Bill] Clinton to work out a Palestinian-Israeli deal showed not only the limits of U.S. influence but also how such influence can backfire and create incentives for the parties to harden their positions. By placing the United States at the center of the negotiations, Clinton raised undue expectations among Israelis and Palestinians that he could "deliver" the other side. At the same time, the White House made far-reaching commitments—for example, proposing that U.S. troops would help secure the border between Israel and a Palestinian state—that would have drawn America into direct involvement in a bitter ethnic-religious war. Such an entanglement would have made the U.S. intervention in Lebanon in the 1980s seem like a pleasure outing. At day's end, the dramatic collapse of the Clinton effort made a bad situation worse while eroding U.S. prestige in the region.

The earlier [peace] talks in Oslo were more successful in moving Palestinians and Israelis toward peace, resulting in a framework agreement that provided a basis for reconciliation. One reason was that the United States played almost no role in the negotiations. Instead, that process involved direct talks between Israeli and Palestinian officials who recognized that only a step-by-step diplomatic course implemented through a combination of confidence building and improvisation could bring about progress.

"Well, it was very nice meeting all of you,
Peace-Lovers from the Middle East!"

That negotiations haven't yet led to the Promised Land of peace shouldn't come as a shock. And it has nothing to do with lack of "U.S. leadership" but rather with the lack of leadership on the Israeli and Palestinian sides. No one should expect that a national conflict, with deep ethnic and religious roots, could be resolved in a week of talks in Camp David. And getting Washington to "do something" is not going to transform this reality.

A Regional Solution

What the United States could do is encourage its friends in the Middle East—Saudi Arabia, Egypt and Jordan—to play more assertive roles in the Palestinian-Israeli conflict. As it is, they are lounging on the diplomatic sidelines and pressing the United States to get involved, or worse, placing obstacles on the road to peace by discouraging the Palestinians from making concessions on Jerusalem. Those Arab countries have not only benefited from American financial largesse and security protection; they know that a collapse of Israeli-Palestinian negotiations could threaten them directly.

At a minimum, the continuing bloodshed in the West Bank could create disorder among the Palestinian population in Jordan and lead to Iraqi intervention in that country. At worst, it could bring about the collapse of peace accords between Israel and both Jordan and Egypt and create the conditions for a regional war.

There are many ways in which Saudi Arabia, Egypt and Jordan, as well as other U.S. "friends" in North Africa and the Persian Gulf, could contribute to a resolution of the conflict. Jordan and Egypt could provide direct support for an Israeli-Palestinian agreement (including an offer to station peacekeeping troops in the West Bank and Gaza). Saudi Arabia and Morocco could propose ideas for Arab control of the Moslem religious sites in Jerusalem. The Saudis and other Gulf states could back the establishment of a regional investment fund to help settle the Palestinian refugees in the West Bank and Jordan. The EU [European Union], whose members, especially France and the Mediterranean states, are more affected by developments in the Middle East than in the Balkans, should assist such efforts.

With a little help from its Middle East and European friends, Washington could start lowering its high-profile role in the region. That change would benefit both the United States and the region.

Periodical Bibliography

The following articles have been selected to supplement the diverse views presented in this chapter.

Mary Bader
"Time for U.S. to Examine Friendship with Israel; Justice Needed for Arabs as Well as Jews," *National Catholic Reporter*, March 29, 2002.

William J. Bennett
"Moral Clarity and the Middle East," *National Review Online*, July 22, 2003. www.nationalreview.com

Allan C. Brownfeld
"Unofficial Agreements Show That, with Support, Peace Is Possible," *Washington Report on Middle East Affairs*, January/February 2004.

Mona Charen
"American Conservatives Are Israel's Staunchest Supporters," *Insight on the News*, May 27, 2002.

Tom DeLay
"Be Not Afraid," *National Review Online*, July 30, 2003. www.nationalreview.com.

Detroit News
"America Should Support Israel's War on Terrorism," December 4, 2001.

David Duke
"The Big Lie: The True Reason Behind the Attack of September 11," www.davidduke.com, October 8, 2001.

David R. Francis
"Economist Tallies Swelling Cost of Israel to U.S.," *Christian Science Monitor*, December 9, 2002.

Reem Haddad
"Bitter, Bitter Tears," *New Internationalist*, November 2001.

Victor Davis Hanson
"Why Support Israel?" *National Review Online*, February 4, 2002. www.nationalreview.com.

Margot Patterson
"When Does a 'Special Relationship' Become a Blank Check to Israel?" *National Catholic Reporter*, April 12, 2002.

For Further Discussion

Chapter 1

1. Yaron Brook and Peter Schwartz argue that because it is a democracy, Israel is the only legitimate state in the Middle East. Do you agree that Israel merits special status due to its political structure? After reading Ahron Cohen, do you believe Israel is a true democracy for all its citizens?

2. The authors of the Kinneret Agreement reaffirm the Jewish nature of Israel. Compare religious states to secular ones. Does each have strengths and weaknesses? Explain. After reading Joel Kovel, do you believe a religious state can be a democracy?

3. Tony Judt believes that the notion of a Jewish state is outdated and that Israel should be binational. Jonathan Rosenblum, however, argues that a binational Israel would resemble a divided state such as Yugoslavia was. Do you believe a Jewish/Islamic state would flourish? Why or why not?

Chapter 2

1. James Inhofe contends that Israel deserves the land of Palestine because Jewish people inhabited the land thousands of years ago. Do you believe this is a valid argument that justifies the creation of the state of Israel?

2. The Islamic Association for Palestine claims that because Palestine has been under Muslim control for most of modern history, the land rightly belongs to the Palestinians. Compare and contrast this argument with Inhofe's. On what basis should land ownership be decided?

3. Paul Eisen claims that Zionism is by its very nature racist, and Israel is therefore a racist state. Barry H. Block claims that Zionism is a liberation movement of an oppressed people. What are the strengths of each argument? Do you think there is validity to each viewpoint?

4. Jonathan Rosenblum claims that all Palestinians are potential terrorists. Patrick Johnston, however, argues that the Israeli government is a terrorist state. Do you think terrorism can be consistently defined, or is it in the eye of the beholder? Explain.

Chapter 3

1. Ziad Asali believes that a peaceful solution to the Israeli-Palestinian conflict can be achieved if both sides compromise. David Horowitz, however, argues that the Palestinians do not want compromise—they want the destruction of Israel. Do you

believe a peaceful solution to the conflict is possible? Is Horowitz's analysis of the Palestinians' motives persuasive?

2. George W. Bush states that the creation of a Palestinian state will bring peace to the region. Has the president's refusal to meet with PLO chairman Yasir Arafat helped or hindered the peace process? Explain.

3. Don Feder contends that Jordan is the only Palestinian state needed. He argues that another Arab state hostile to Israel would lead to the end of Israel. Is Feder's argument convincing? Why or why not?

4. Uzi Landau argues that the only way for Israel to protect itself from terrorists is to construct a security fence. Catherine Cook contends that the fence is part of Israel's illegal annexation of Palestinian land. Since the beginning of the construction of the fence, terrorist attacks in Israel have declined sharply. Does this fact justify the fence's encroachment on Palestinian land? Why or why not?

Chapter 4

1. Bruce S. Thornton states that America should continue to support Israel because it is a democracy, but Sarah Helm contends that America's support of Israel breeds Muslim resentment and terrorism. Which argument is more compelling? Why?

2. According to Paul Findley, terrorists attacked America on September 11, 2001, because of America's support for Israel. Do you believe the terrorist threat would decline if America withdrew its support for Israel? Why or why not?

3. Lee H. Hamilton argues that in order to resolve the Middle East conflict, the United States must intervene. In light of the failure of most U.S. peacemaking efforts to date, how convincing is Hamilton's argument?

4. Leon Hadar contends that the Israeli-Palestinian conflict is a regional one that should be solved by the region's nations, not the United States. Do you believe a regional solution is possible, or must Europe, the United Nations, or the United States intervene?

Chronology

63 B.C.– A.D. 313	Palestine is ruled by the Romans.
313–636	The Byzantine Empire rules Palestine.
636–1099	Palestine is ruled by Arabs.
1099–1291	Crusaders dominate Palestine.
1291–1516	The Mamluk rule Palestine.
1517–1917	The Ottoman Empire rules Palestine.
1839	Moses Montefiore, a British Jew, calls for the creation of a Jewish state.
1882–1903	The first aliyah (large-scale Jewish immigration to Palestine) occurs.
1896	Theodor Herzl publishes *Der Judenstat*, which leads to the formation of the World Zionist Congress.
1904–1914	The second aliyah occurs.
1909	Tel Aviv is founded; it is the first modern all-Jewish city in Palestine.
1917	The British conquer Palestine. The British foreign minister declares support for the establishment of a "Jewish national home in Palestine."
1917–1948	The British rule over Palestine.
1919–1923	The third aliyah occurs.
1922	The League of Nations grants Britain a mandate for Palestine.
1924–1932	The fourth aliyah occurs.
1929–1939	Arabs rebel against British rule. Intense fighting between Jews and Arabs ensues.
1933–1939	The fifth aliyah occurs.
1939–1945	The Holocaust occurs in Europe during World War II.

1947	The United Nations votes to partition Palestine into a Jewish state and an Arab state.
1948	The British Mandate ends on May 14, and the state of Israel is declared the same day. On May 15, five Arab nations invade Israel. More than five hundred thousand Arabs flee Israel.
1948–1952	Massive Jewish emigration from Europe and Arab countries occurs.
1949	Israel signs armistice agreements with Egypt, Jordan, Syria, and Lebanon and is admitted to the United Nations.
1967	The Six-Day War occurs. Israel attacks Egypt, Syria, and Jordan and occupies East Jerusalem, the West Bank, Golan Heights, Gaza, and Sinai Peninsula. The UN Security Council adopts resolution 242, which calls for Israel to return the land it acquired in the Six-Day War and for Arab nations to respect Israel's boundaries.
1973	The Yom Kippur War begins. Egypt and Syria launch a surprise attack against Israel. After three weeks of Arab gains, Israel, with American support, defeats the attackers.
1979	Israel and Egypt sign a peace treaty.
1981	The Israeli air force destroys Iraq's nuclear reactor days before it is to go online. Israel suspected Iraq of developing a nuclear weapons program.
1982	In keeping with the 1979 treaty with Egypt, Israel completes its withdrawal from the Sinai Peninsula.
1989	Mass emigration from the Soviet Union to Israel occurs.
1991	Israel is struck with Iraqi missiles during the Gulf War; at the request of the United States, Israel does not retaliate.
1992	Israel establishes diplomatic relations with India and China.

1994	The Palestinian Authority assumes governing authority in Gaza and Jericho. Israel and Jordan sign a peace treaty.
1995	Prime Minister Yitzhak Rabin is assassinated at a peace rally.
1998	Israel celebrates the fiftieth anniversary of its founding.
2003	In response to terrorism Israel begins the construction of a massive security fence to separate Israel from the West Bank. The fence is widely condemned around the world, but terrorist attacks on Israeli soil decrease significantly as a result of its construction.
2004	Yassir Arafat dies.

Organizations to Contact

The editors have compiled the following list of organizations concerned with the issues debated in this book. The descriptions are derived from materials provided by the organizations. All have publications or information available for interested readers. The list was compiled on the date of publication of the present volume; the information provided here may change. Be aware that many organizations take several weeks or longer to respond to inquiries, so allow as much time as possible.

American-Israeli Cooperative Enterprise (AICE)
2810 Blaine Dr., Chevy Chase, MD 20815
(301) 565-3918 • fax: (301) 587-9056
e-mail: mgbard@aol.com • Web site: www.us-israel.org

AICE seeks to strengthen the U.S.-Israel relationship by emphasizing values the two nations have in common and developing cooperative social and educational programs that address shared domestic problems. It also works to enhance Israel's image by publicizing novel Israeli solutions to these problems. It published the book *Partners for Change: How U.S.-Israel Cooperation Can Benefit America*. Its Web site includes the Jewish Virtual Library, a comprehensive online encyclopedia of Jewish history.

American Jewish Committee (AJC)
PO Box 705, New York, NY 10150
(212) 751-4000 • fax: (212) 838-2120
e-mail: PR@ajc.org • Web site: www.ajc.org

AJC works to strengthen U.S.-Israel relations, build international support for Israel, and support the Israeli-Arab peace process. The committee's numerous publications include the *AJC Journal*, the report *Muslim Anti-Semitism: A Clear and Present Danger*, and the papers "Iran and the Palestinian War Against Israel" and "The Arab Campaign to Destroy Israel."

Americans for Middle East Understanding (AMEU)
475 Riverside Dr., Room 245, New York, NY 10115-0245
(212) 870-2053 • fax: (212) 870-2050
e-mail: info@ameu.org • Web site: www.ameu.org

AMEU's purpose is to foster a better understanding in America of the history, goals, and values of Middle Eastern cultures and peoples, the rights of Palestinians, and the forces shaping U.S. policy in the Middle East. AMEU publishes *The Link*, a bimonthly newsletter, as well as books and pamphlets on the Middle East.

Foundation for Middle East Peace
1763 N St. NW, Washington, DC 20036
(202) 835-3650 • fax: (202) 835-3651
e-mail: info@fmep.org • Web site: www.fmep.org

The foundation assists the peaceful resolution of the Israeli-Palestinian conflict by making financial grants available within the Arab and Jewish communities. It publishes the bimonthly *Report on Israeli Settlements in the Occupied Territories* and additional books and papers.

Israel Democracy Institute
PO Box 4702, Jerusalem 91046 Israel
02-530-0888 • fax: 02-530-0837
Web site: www.idi.org.il

This organization is an independent nonpartisan research institute. It was founded in 1991 as a center for policy studies, straddling the spheres of politics and academia, the world of decision makers and the world of thinkers in Israel. Its numerous publications can be ordered from its catalog, which is available online or by mail.

Middle East Forum
1500 Walnut St., Suite 1050, Philadelphia, PA 19102
(215) 546-5406 • fax: (215) 546-5409
e-mail: info@meforum.org • Web site: www.meforum.org

The Middle East Forum is a think tank that works to define and promote American interests in the Middle East. It supports strong American ties with Israel, Turkey, and other democracies as they emerge. It publishes the *Middle East Quarterly*, a policy-oriented journal. Its Web site includes articles, summaries of activities, and a discussion forum.

U.S. Department of State, Bureau of Near Eastern Affairs
2201 C St. NW, Washington, DC 20520
(202) 647-4000
Web site: www.state.gov

The bureau deals with U.S. foreign policy and U.S. relations with the countries in the Middle East and North Africa, including Israel. Its Web site offers country information as well as news briefings and press statements on U.S. foreign policy.

Washington Institute for Near East Policy
1828 L St. NW, Suite 1050, Washington, DC 20036
(202) 452-0650 • fax: (202) 223-5364
e-mail: info@washingtoninstitute.org
Web site: www.washingtoninstitute.org
The institute is an independent, nonprofit research organization that provides information and analysis on the Middle East and U.S. policy in the region. It publishes numerous books, periodic monographs, and reports on regional politics, security, and economics, including *PeaceWatch*, which focuses on the Arab-Israeli peace process, and the reports *Democracy and Arab Political Culture* and *Radical Middle East States and U.S. Policy*.

World Jewish Congress
PO Box 90400, Washington, DC 20090
e-mail: info@worldjewishcongress.org
Web site: www.worldjewishcongress.org
The World Jewish Congress is an international organization whose mission is to address the interests and needs of Jews and Jewish communities throughout the world. It publishes *Dispatches*, *Policy Forum*, and *Policy Studies*, which provide brief critical articles on current topics.

Zionist Organization of America
4 E. Thirty-fourth St., New York, NY 10016
(212) 481-1500 • fax: (212) 481-1515
e-mail: info@zoa.org • Web site: www.zoa.org
This organization is the oldest, and one of the largest, pro-Israel organizations in the United States. Its many publications can be downloaded from the Web site.

Web Sites

Bitterlemons.org
www.bitterlemons.org
This Web site presents Israeli and Palestinian viewpoints on the Palestinian-Israeli conflict and peace process as well as related regional issues of concern.

HAARETZ.com
www.haaretzdaily.com
This is an online edition of one of the leading Israeli newspapers published in English.

Israel Ministry of Foreign Affairs

www.mfa.gov.il

This official Israeli government site describes the government's policies and relations with other countries.

Jerusalem Post

www.jpost.com

This is the online edition of the daily Jerusalem newspaper.

MidEastWeb

www.mideastweb.org

MidEastWeb is a Web site founded by people from different nations who are active in peace education efforts. Its Web site features articles and opinions about events in the region, as well as maps and a history of the conflict in the Middle East.

Palestinian National Authority

www.pna.gov

The official Web site of the Palestinian National Authority, the organization in charge of Palestinian-administered areas of the West Bank and Gaza Strip.

Bibliography of Books

Said K. Aburish — *Arafat: From Defender to Dictator.* London: Bloomsbury USA, 1999.

Ian Black with Benny Morris — *Israel's Secret Wars: A History of Israel's Intelligence Services.* New York: Grove/Atlantic, 1992.

John Bright — *History of Israel.* Phoenix, AZ: Westminster John Knox Press, 2000.

Noam Chomsky — *Fateful Triangle: The United States, Israel, and the Palestinians.* Cambridge, MA: South End Press, 1999.

Noam Chomsky — *Middle East Illusions: Including Peace in the Middle East? Reflections on Justice and Nationhood.* Lanham, MD: Rowman & Littlefield, 2003.

Richard Ben Cramer — *How Israel Lost: The Four Questions.* New York: Simon & Schuster, 2004.

Alan Dershowitz — *The Case for Israel.* Hoboken, NJ: John Wiley & Sons, 2003.

Noah J. Efron — *Real Jews: Secular Versus Ultra-Orthodox: The Struggle for Jewish Identity in Israel.* New York: Basic Books, 2003.

Norman G. Finkelstein — *Image and Reality of the Israel-Palestine Conflict.* New York: W.W. Norton, 2003.

Martin Gilbert — *The Jews in the Twentieth Century: An Illustrated History.* New York: Schocken Books, 2001.

Martin Gilbert — *The Routledge Atlas of Arab-Israeli Conflict: The Complete History of the Struggle and the Efforts to Resolve It.* London: Routledge, 2002.

Arthur Hertzberg — *The Fate of Zionism: A Secular Future for Israel and Palestine.* New York: HarperCollins, 2003.

Theodor Herzl — *The Jewish State.* Mineola, NY: Dover, 1989.

David Horowitz — *Still Life with Bombers: Israel in the Age of Terrorism.* New York: Knopf, 2004.

Efraim Karsh — *Arafat's War: The Man and His Battle for Israeli Conquest.* New York: Grove Press, 2003.

Baruch Kimmerling — *The Palestinian People: A History.* Cambridge, MA: Harvard University Press, 2003.

Walter Laqueur — *A History of Zionism: From the French Revolution to the Establishment of the State of Israel.* New York: Random House, 2003.

Yaacov Lozowick	*Right to Exist: A Moral Defense of Israel's Wars.* New York: Doubleday, 2003.
Benny Morris	*Righteous Victims: A History of the Zionist-Arab Conflict, 1881–1999.* New York: Alfred A. Knopf, 2001.
Jo-Ann Mort and Gary Brenner	*Our Hearts Invented a Place: Can Kibbutzim Survive in Today's Israel?* Ithaca, NY: Cornell University Press, 2003.
Benjamin Netanyahu	*A Durable Peace: Israel and Its Place Among the Nations.* New York: Warner Books, 2000.
Michael B. Oren	*Six Days of War: June 1967 and the Making of the Modern Middle East.* New York: Ballantine Books, 2003.
Ilan Pappe	*A History of Modern Palestine: One Land, Two Peoples.* Cambridge, UK: Cambridge University Press, 2003.
Joan Peters	*From Time Immemorial: The Origins of the Arab-Jewish Conflict over Palestine.* Chicago: JKAP, 1993.
Abraham Rabinovich	*The Yom Kippur War: The Epic Encounter That Transformed the Middle East.* New York: Schocken Books; 2004.
Tanya Reinhart	*Israel/Palestine: How to End the War of 1948.* New York: Seven Stories Press, 2002.
Donna Rosenthal	*The Israelis: Ordinary People in an Extraordinary Land.* New York: Free Press, 2003.
Joe Sacco	*Palestine.* Seattle: Fantagraphics Books, 2001.
Howard M. Sacharm	*A History of Israel: From the Rise of Zionism to Our Time.* New York: Random House, 1996.
Edward W. Said	*The Question of Palestine.* New York: Knopf, 1992.
Tom Segev and Arlen Neal Weinstein	*1949: The First Israelis.* New York: Owl Books, 1998.
Israel Shahak and Norton Mezvinsky	*Jewish Fundamentalism in Israel.* London: Pluto Press, 2004.
David K. Shipler	*Arab and Jew: Wounded Spirits in a Promised Land.* New York: Penguin Books, 2002.
Avi Shlaim	*Iron Wall: Israel and the Arab World.* New York: W.W. Norton, 2000.
Charles D. Smith	*Palestine and the Arab-Israeli Conflict.* New York: Bedford Books, 2000.
Leslie Stein	*The Hope Fulfilled: The Rise of Modern Israel.* Westport, CT: Praeger, 2003.

Baylis Thomas

How Israel Was Won: A Concise History of the Arab-Israeli Conflict. Lanham, MD: Lexington Books, 1999.

Tony Walker and Andrew Gowers

Arafat: The Biography. London: Virgin Books, 2003.

Keith W. Whitelam

The Invention of Ancient Israel: The Silencing of Palestinian History. London: Routledge, 1997.

Sigalit Zetouni, Anita Miller, and Jordan Miller

Sharon: Israel's Warrior-Politician. Chicago: Academy Chicago & Olive Publishing, 2002.

Index

Abbas, Mahmoud, 131
Abdullah (prince), 60
Afghanistan, 105
agriculture, 64
Ahadith of Prophet Muhammad, 72
Al-Akhbar (newspaper), 176
Al-Aksa Martyrs Brigade, 94
Ala, Abu, 142
Alfe Menashe (West Bank), 148–49
aliyahs, 14–15
Allenby, Edmund, 61–62
anti-Americanism, 173–74, 176
anti-Semitism
    Palestinian, 24, 119–20, 132, 142
    Western, 46, 50, 86–87
    Zionism and, 42, 85
Arab League, 117
Arabs
    deny Israel's right to exist, 69, 88,
      95–96, 117–18, 124, 159
    effect of Palestinian issue on, 112
    Israeli
      are citizens, 87–88
      birthrate of, 15
      human rights of, are respected, 33
      in occupied territories, 45–46
      live peacefully, 142
      most, immigrated after Jews, 63–64
      population of, dooms binational
        state, 52
    rejected partition, 24, 57, 88, 156
    reject peace, 67–69, 117
    removal of, from Israel, 16
    teach hatred of Jews, 119–20
    see also Palestinians
Arab states
    are not democracies, 136
    created Palestinian problem, 123
    deny human rights, 53
    must recognize Israel's right to exist,
      179–80
    treated refugees badly, 119, 121
    were created by Western nations, 64,
      105, 133
    see also specific Arab states
Arafat, Yasir
    birthplace, 121
    denies Israeli right to exist, 60, 95–96
    is dictator, 23
    is patron of terrorism, 21–22, 92–95,
      123, 134–35
    Israeli actions against, 99
    on Palestinian birthrate as weapon,
      15
    plan of, to defeat Israel, 133

    PLO goals and, 117
    rejects peace, 67–69, 88–89, 122, 164
    removal of, 131
    supports Iraq, 132
archaeology, 60–61
Asali, Ziad, 107
Awkil, Nabil, 175
Ayalon, Daniel, 140
Azam, Abdallah, 175

Badawi, Naser, 94
Baitul-Maqdis, 72–73, 75
Balfour Declaration, 63, 74, 155
Barak, Ehud, 88–89, 122, 140, 164
Ben-Gurion, David, 14, 18, 78, 156
Bennett, William J., 175
Bible, 67
binational state, 15
    should be instituted, 47, 51–52
    con, 52–54
bin Laden, Osama, 165, 170, 173–75
Block, Barry H., 83
Boland, Sue, 28
Brinkley, Joel, 94
British Mandate, 57, 117, 156
Brook, Yaron, 20
Brownfeld, Allan C., 40
B'tselem (Israeli human rights
    organization), 146, 147, 149
Burg, Avraham, 52
Bush, George H.W., 66
Bush, George W., 125
    foreign policy of, 182
    policies of, toward Israel, 91, 99, 163,
      171, 178
    al Qaeda and, 100
    relationship of, with Sharon, 170
    Road Map and, 112–13, 131
    sees Israel as natural ally, 159
    terrorism policy of, 164–65

Camp David peace treaty, 139
Central Conference of American
    Rabbis, 88
Cheney, Dick, 166
Christianity, 73–74
Christison, Bill, 81
Christison, Kathleen, 81
Clemens, Samuel, 63
Clinton, Bill, 88–89, 164, 182
Cohen, Ahron, 26
Commentary (magazine), 135
Cook, Catherine, 143

democracy/democratic

Voltaire, 64

wars, 66, 75, 105
Washington Post (newspaper), 93, 164, 173
water, 145
weapon of the womb, 15, 16
Weitzman, Chaim, 63, 78
West Bank
  annexation of, 15, 168
  conditions in, 168
  Intifada in, 75
  is necessary for defense of Israel, 134, 135, 139
  self-governing authority of, was granted by Israel, 122
  was controlled by Jordan, 117
  see also occupied territories; settlements
Western civilization
  Islam is at war with, 75

Israel represents, 22, 158, 159
Palestinians resent, 121
Wilson, A.N., 50
Wine, Sherwin, 52
World War I, 61–63
World War II, 57, 64–65, 155

Zionism
  anti-Semitism and, 42
  background of, 31, 45, 51, 57
  created only democracy in Middle East, 86
  goal of, 14, 78
  international endorsements of, 84
  is imperialist, 38
  is liberation movement, 86–87
  is racist, 40, 41–43, 78–79, 81, 84, 85
    con, 50, 85–89
  is threat to Judaism, 27, 29
  Truman supported, 155
Zogby, James, 179